Creative Lettering Today

MICHAEL HARVEY

Creative Lettering Today

CALLIGRAPHY IN THE GRAPHIC ARTS

DRAWING AND DESIGN

DIGITAL LETTERFORMS

CARVING LETTERS IN STONE AND WOOD

A & C Black · London

First published 1996 in the UK by
A & C Black (Publishers) Limited
35 Bedford Row, London WC1R 4JH

ISBN 0-7136-4576-8

Originally published 1996 in the USA by
Design Books, distributed by Lyons & Burford, Publishers
31 West 21st Street, New York NY 10010

© 1996, 1988, 1987, 1985 by Michael Harvey

Creative Lettering Today brings together three previously published titles:
Calligraphy in the Graphic Arts, *Drawing and Design* and
Carving Letters in Stone and Wood
in addition to new material.

A CIP catalogue record for this book is available from the British Library.

Production Ken Gross
Printed in the United States of America
by Edwards Brothers, Lillington, North Carolina

Contents

Introduction 7

Historical background 10

Introduction

The adjective 'creative' in the title of this book perhaps needs defining so that the reader is not misled into expecting an especially *avant garde* or experimental approach to the subject. Many years ago a teaching job I applied for specified the ability to teach 'roman and creative lettering'. I was puzzled by this because I had been carving roman letters in stone and drawing lettered bookjackets for several years and thought of both activities as creative work. Whoever drafted the job description perhaps thought of roman lettering as a necessary discipline – which it is – and creative lettering as fancy, unconventional or even distorted – which it is not necessarily. Perhaps they meant 'expressionist' or 'artistic'? My feeling then in 1961 was that all lettering should be more or less creative, depending on the use to which it is put, and after continuing to practice lettering in several fields I feel the same today. Creativity is an approach, an attitude, to design, and the lettering designer uses skill, artistry, imagination and judgement to serve the particular demands of each job. Inventiveness, even when daring, will be held in check by considerations of legibility, convention and a sense of fitness for purpose. This wider meaning of creativity underlies the purpose and argument of the present book.

This volume brings together three books written between 1985 and 1988 that, at the time, I considered covered the 'trinity of the letter-making arts': calligraphy, drawing and carving. Since 1992 I have been working on a Macintosh computer, designing digital typefaces, and now it seems that the trinity must make way for the quartet, so this book has a quarter of its pages devoted to digital lettering.

Five hundred years ago, when the manuscript book was central to our culture, calligraphy was *the* graphic art, but the advent of the printed book removed the broad-edged pen from its central, creative role as a letter-making instrument, and today the written letter is only one of the elements that may be employed in a graphic designer's repertoire. That calligraphy – a fairly recent term – survives today is largely due to the revival, mostly amateur, that began in England in the early years of this century when Edward Johnston's classes at the Central School of Arts and Crafts in London attracted many enthusiastic students. This revival has recently gathered strength from America, where calligraphic societies now abound and much original and creative work is done. Until recently calligraphy was part of the education of students of art and design, but has since been dropped from all but a few colleges because it was felt to have no purpose today, when typefaces seem to fulfil every need. This view ignored the unique educational ability of calligraphy to provide understanding of the forms from which type derives, or its creative use where the limitations of type hamper the designer's vision. In the first section of this book calligraphic form is explained from a graphic designer's perspective, with the aim to encourage, through the use of calligraphic tools, both an understanding of form and a desire for creative experiment.

Lettering is a kind of drawing in which forms, originally calligraphic, are remade, adapted and developed for non-written purposes. Drawing with a pointed tool such as a pencil produces lines which lack the substance of those flowing from the scribe's broad-edged pen, leading naturally to letters in outline which can be filled in, left open or easily erased and redrawn. Thus the letterer has an advantage over the calligrapher who, having written, must move on or start again. The lettering designer working at the drawing board is able to plan characters carefully, modifying their proportions, adding or subtracting weight. By drawing they can be given a special flavour, a *drawn* character. This controlled freedom can be developed until drawing becomes the major shaping force in the letterforms. The relationship between written and drawn letterforms can be very close or almost non-existent. When preparing the illustrations that appear on pages 70 to 75 in section two, I first made many photographs of my hand drawing letters so that I could understand myself what had become an almost automatic process. This was a revelation and confirmed my view that an individual's fingers are able to produce letterforms with a personal character. In a very real sense the letters I made were *mine*, and my belief is that making individual letters is open to anyone prepared to put in the time to discover their hand's abilities.

Drawn letters, for many years the most refined representatives of our Western lettering culture, in the sense that drawing lies behind the most elegant typefaces and inscriptions, are now dismissed as 'analogue'. In today's digital world any form that is not able to be read by a computer is felt to be somehow merely a step on the way to the ideal, the digital letter. Technology once again steps in. Since Gutenberg's time calligraphy has been sidelined, and now with the rise of the computer and digital type drawing itself becomes the handmaiden of the new technology. Now, computer typefaces range right across the last two-thousand years, bringing us on the one hand a faithful translation of the Trajan letter from the first century of our era, to the wildest, most idiosyncratic contemporary scripts. Almost everything we read now uses computer-generated type, arranged on the page with a software program. Unlike writing, drawing and carving, in which hand, tools and materials affect the shapes of letters, the computer's influence is nil. It can of course, as is seen every day, produce distortions and other gimmicks, but not in these pages. At first, digital letters were clumsy compromises that offended the eyes of all but computer engineers, but only a few years on they rival the very best work of the past on which our ideas of quality rest.

The computer is now a familiar tool in most design studios, and in those of many home-based calligraphers and designers. With specific software all can now attempt to design typefaces, and what was previously an almost secret, technologically remote process, is now open to anyone with a Macintosh and enough patience and determination. The third section of this book is a guide to this exciting journey.

Through the permanence of stone we still have the sublime capital letters of the Romans in our possession, a source of inspiration at the Renaissance and again in this century. Nothing could be a greater contrast to today's immaterial, digital letters than those that are carved in stone with mallet and chisel, but today the carved letter is still very much with us. Like the twentieth-century revival of calligraphy, this era's new-found interest in inscriptional lettering can be traced back to one man, Eric Gill, himself a pupil and friend of Edward Johnston. From Gill's example a school of craftsmen has emerged in England, specialising for the most part in elegant and restrained memorials in stone, while in Germany a rather more vigorous and adventurous attitude to the carved letter is evident.

Although the roman capital is considered the inscriptional letter par excellence, there is no need for the carver today to be limited to that particular form. Later, typographic letters with their subtly changed stroke weights, proportions and serifs are excellent models for carving. The chisel can equally well incise other forms, such as lowercase and script letters; indeed, copperplate scripts lend themselves so naturally to the chisel that one wonders whether the Roman carvers would have used these forms if they had been available. Bold letters with strong serifs, letters with no serifs at all, the chisel has no preferences, even though the carver might. Chisels are simply tools for removing waste material and have little influence on letterforms. The carver, driving a chisel into stone (or wood), knowing the particular qualities of the material, carves the letter that he has in his mind's eye, remembering Hermann Zapf's liberating statement: it's all a question of what you want.

The final section of this book describes the various techniques for carving letters in wood and stone, then concentrates on the design of gravestones and memorials. This is an important field, a source of commissions for the professional, where a conservative approach is usually adopted or preferred by clients, but, as these pages show, such designs do not have to be dull or uniform. Other fields allow for more ambitious work, such as one of the largest carving commissions in England that is described here. Finally, an example of lettering in wood treated as sculpture underlines the fact that every piece of carved lettering, whether incised or relief, is indeed a form of sculpture.

The reader of this book will soon become aware that although it is in four separate sections dealing with very different aspects of lettering today, these are far from being watertight compartments, as the forms seen in one section will appear again in another. This reflects the author's long experience of working in all these fields, but also illustrates the fact that the culture of letters as practiced today is very rich, that there is no longer a fixed idea of what good lettering is. Anyone who now suggests that a particular style is the best will sound very old-fashioned indeed, although it was not long ago that the letters on the base of the Trajan column in Rome were held up as an ideal form. The puritanism of the revivalist period has passed and we can now enjoy a whole variety of letterforms from every period, reviving them, editing them, translating them into our visual language and technologies, making them work for us in our very complex world. This is not mere pastiche but rather a sign of healthy interest in a rich artform. We are less interested in knowing which form would suit a particular circumstance in some conventional way, but rather seek to discover the form that would work best while also surprising and exciting us. We know the rules, we break the rules, we make up new rules and then break those too. There are fashions in lettering, and everyone but the most isolated is influenced by fashion. Revivals continue. For a while the calligraphic renaissance seemed to be everywhere, then it was 1920's geometric letters that looked so cool after all that broad pen swooping and curling. In the end the designer has to choose, for in a world in which almost everything is available, design becomes largely a matter of choice. What will *really* work here, the designer asks. I hope that this book will help readers find some of the answers.

Michael Harvey, Bridport, 1996

For permission to reproduce designs the author wishes to thank the following:
Adobe Systems; Allen Lane; B. V. Uitgeverij de Arbeiderpers; The Bodley Head; Centre de Recherches en Esthétique Appliquée; Cambridge University Press; the estate of E. M. Catich; Dancing Inks; English National Opera; Ian Hamilton Finlay; E. M. Querido's Uitgeverij B. V.; Tate Gallery Publications; The Thimble Press; Richard Calvocoressi; Pat England; Barbara Gathercole; Lyn Gathercole; Graham C. Greene; Lulu Minguet; Monotype Typography; John Neal; Van Nostrand Reinhold Company; Hugh and Jane Roberts; Mrs Janet Stone; Hermann Zapf; and the estate of George Bernard Shaw for the quotation on page 35. The author also wishes to thank especially Will Carter for generously divulging his knife carving technique, John Ryder who was closely involved with three of the books that are included in this volume, Carol Twombly and Linnea Lundquist for their advice on the Digital Lettering section, and Richard Smith for the photographs of the author on page 217.

Historical background

Anyone working with letters needs to know something of their historical development, and this is especially relevant with carved lettering because the inscriptional Roman capital is the foundation of all western letterforms and is still a measure of excellence. The alphabet that the Romans evolved from earlier Greek and Phoenician forms has a geometric structure underpinning strokes of varying width that end in the elegant terminals called serifs. Carved into stone around two thousand years ago these letters survived to inspire Renaissance scholars, architects and printers and remain a source of study and inspiration today. A square-cut brush was used to write out the inscription before carving and evidence of the brush's modelling of the geometric forms is seen clearly in the first century BC fragment from the Roman Forum shown here. Research by E. M. Catich (see page 221), once a Chicago signwriter, is very convincing on the part that the brush played in Roman inscriptional lettering, as his brush-written Imperial capitals, below, demonstrate.

Although the brush shaped the letters the chisel tidied up the written character where necessary, particularly at junctions and serifs.

ADEGLARVN
SPQR

SERVMINTERAA

SPERARE

euoaugeliu

II

As Rome declined, the manuscript book spread the Christian faith through Europe, developing many new scripts in which the round forms that suit writing often predominate. The main scripts are shown here, at left. A relaxed, compressed form of capital called *rustic* of around the fourth century is followed by *uncial* and *half-uncial* of the fifth and sixth centuries. Below, the *minuscule* script of the ninth century, and, bottom right, the style generally called *blackletter* from the fifteenth century, here in the condensed, angular *textura* form, and bottom left, *italic* from the sixteenth-century manual of Arrighi. The latter two examples, in which flourishes embellish the lettering, are from printed woodcuts.

Quaepoſtquam geſtaſunt . temptauitdſabraham . &dixitadeu · Abraham . illereſpondit · Adſu · Artilli· Tollefiliumtuum unigentui quemdilu giſiſaac . &uadeinterrauiſionis atq: offer eum

Graue'fatica non ti fia ad imparar fare' le'
littere' Maiuſcule', quando nelle' pic=
cole'harai firmato bene'
la mano, et
eo maxime' ch'io ti ho
diſto che' li Dui principij delle'
Piccole' ſonno anchora quelli delle' Grandi
come' continuando il ſcriuere', da te
medeſimo uenerai
cognoſcendo
Non ti diro adunque' altro, ſaluo che' te'
sforZi' imparar fare' le' tue' Maiuſcule'
Come' qui apreſſo ri=
trouerai per eſſe=
pio deſignato

BIBLIA
SACRA
VVLGATAE
EDITIONIS
TRIBVS TOMIS
DISTINCTA

ROMAE
Ex Typographia Apoſtolica Vaticana
M·D·X·C

Caslon

One of the greatest virtues of
good typography
is unobtrusive elegance

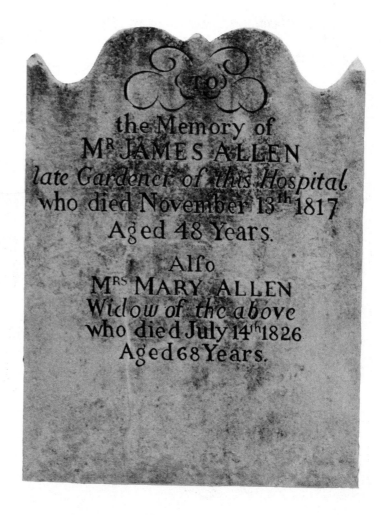

The invention of movable type, involving the shaping of letters on steel punches, a kind of miniature sculpture, and fifteenth-century scholarship established the Roman capital (uppercase) in the new printing technology. A titlepage from 1590, above, shows type symmetrically arranged (an easy task for the printer) and two wood-cut letters from Cresci's *Essemplare*, 1578, show the skill of the Renaissance scribe. Type now set the style in lettering: lowercase, whose forms can be traced back to the tenth-century minuscule script, and italic, a writing style that flourished in the Papal chanceries are represented here by William Caslon's design of 1725, and William Bulmer's italic of around 1790, expressing an ideal that applies equally well to the design of inscriptions.

Many gravestones survive from this period that reflect the style of the printed book's titlepage, such as this late example from the Royal Hospital, Chelsea; an elegant display of names, dates and information using capitals, lowercase and italic in a well articulated design, marred only by the figures which would have been better in the old style form used on the gravestone described on page 196.

Two examples of the revival of lettering and calligraphy in this century are shown here; a rubbing from an inscription by Eric Gill of 1928 in which capitals are tightly packed with diamond-shaped dots separating words, an echo of Roman inscriptional practice (St Bride Library), and a wood-engraved bookplate by Reynolds Stone for Alfred Fairbank, the leader of the revival of italic handwriting. Stone, who was influenced by Gill, also carved italic lettering in slate.

A less traditional approach to design is illustrated below by two examples of the work of Hermann Zapf; a titlepage using lowercase letters in an asymmetrical arrangement and four lines of drawn capitals and figures that range from the left. A study of the work of such contemporary masters will widen the designer's approach to design, providing a rich source of letterforms, textures and arrangements.

The Comedies
and Tragedies
of William
Shakespeare
Complete
and unabridged
with notes and
glossary *
Illustrated by
Fritz Kredel
* Volume II
Random House

IN MEMORIAM

S. FISCHER

24. DEZEMBER

1859 – 1959

1

Calligraphy in the graphic arts

Tools, materials and equipment

Writing and drawing letters requires very little equipment beyond pens, pencils, brushes, ink, paper and a flat surface to work upon. Add to these white paint for re-touching if working for reproduction, a straight-edge and set square (triangle) to ensure accuracy and the lettering designer is in business. Most of the illustrations in the first two sections of this book were made with these tools, but the following detailed list includes other useful items.

Pens for writing Broad-edged fibre-tipped pens in various widths, ideally 'permanent' as these will allow re-touching with white watercolour. Some pens work best after they have been in use for a while, so try to break in a new pen before using it for writing, and remember that a pen near exhaustion may produce letters with an interesting texture. The ink cartridge Artpen has

some of the flexibility that fibre-tipped pens lack, while the Mars Graphic 3000 combines a fine point with considerable flexibility, responding to pressure in a similar way to a brush.

Pens for drawing Pointed fibre-tipped pens in fine to medium thickness are good for sketching designs or, if 'permanent', for drawing letters for reproduction. A black felt marker is useful for filling in large letters and, unlike ink, does not wrinkle the paper. Technical pens such as the Rotring Rapidoliner can be used for drawing or for refining the edges of letters.

Pencils Freehand drawing requires pencils that are soft enough to respond to pressure and hard enough to stay sharp without repeated sharpening. HB and H are good grades for general use, 2B and softer is good for textures and 2H for ruling guide lines.

Brushes Round ended brushes, in sable or nylon, which take a fine point and spread under pressure are suitable for writing brush scripts, while the flat variety works in a similar way to a broad-edged pen, making strokes of varying thickness. Keep one fine brush exclusively for re-touching, and remember that an old battered brush may produce very vigorous letters.

Ink Use black waterproof drawing ink for brush writing or filling in out-lines, remembering to wash brushes afterwards. With metal nibs a non-waterproof ink will produce finer lines.

Paper A fairly smooth surface, not too absorbent, and with a slight rough-ness to help pen control, is best for most calligraphic work. Detail or bond paper in pads is ideal when working with fibre-tipped pens, but avoid papers that cause the pen to bleed. Thicker

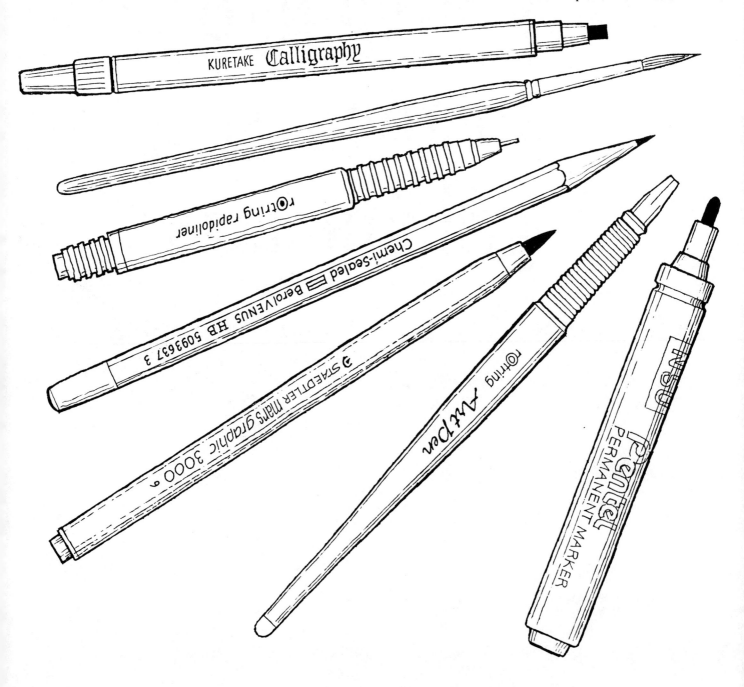

drawing papers with rough surfaces can produce interesting textures in the writing, while very absorbent papers, such as blotting paper, can give unusual effects. Lettering for reproduction may be drawn on line board or paper, such as CS10 or similar, and the thinner detail and tracing papers are useful when working on a lightbox. Another useful material is scraper or scratch board, white for black ink work. Errors can be erased with a sharp knife – a precise alternative to re-touching with a brush. A substantial watercolour paper is essential for preparing designs in gouache colours.

Paint White gouache for re-touching, with black an alternative to ink; its thicker consistency can be used to advantage in expressive writing, and, like ink, it can be thinned with water to make softly toned letters. Coloured

gouache for preparing designs to show clients or for exhibition work.

Adhesives Rubber cement for paste-up work and as a resist medium, a general purpose clear glue and an aerosol spraymounting adhesive.

Other materials and equipment
Scissors and a craft knife; drafting tape; an eraser (keep a large soft brush handy to clear the working surface of eraser debris); crayons (their use as a resist is shown on page 51); paper towels for wiping brushes and pens, but also as an experimental writing surface (see page 50). As well as these sundry items – a list that could grow indefinitely – it is desirable to have a drawing board that can be adjusted to a comfortable angle, a suitable chair and the usual drafting equipment such a protractor and a ruler. Good lighting is essential, but avoid direct sunlight and use an

adjustable lamp when daylight fails, or, even better, a combined lamp and magnifying glass. A reducing glass is useful for assessing the final appearance of work that has been drawn larger than the actual reproduction size. In addition to the equipment listed above the professional lettering designer may have a lightbox or table, a drafting machine attached to either a drawing board or lightbox for extremely accurate drawing, an opaque projector – 'Grant Projector', 'Copyscanner', 'Lucy' machine – for projecting enlarged or reduced images for tracing. He will also have access to a photocopier, a wonderful device, much used in the making of this book. For really first-class reproduction images the process camera was once a necessity, but today digital layout and design software has largely replaced this piece of equipment.

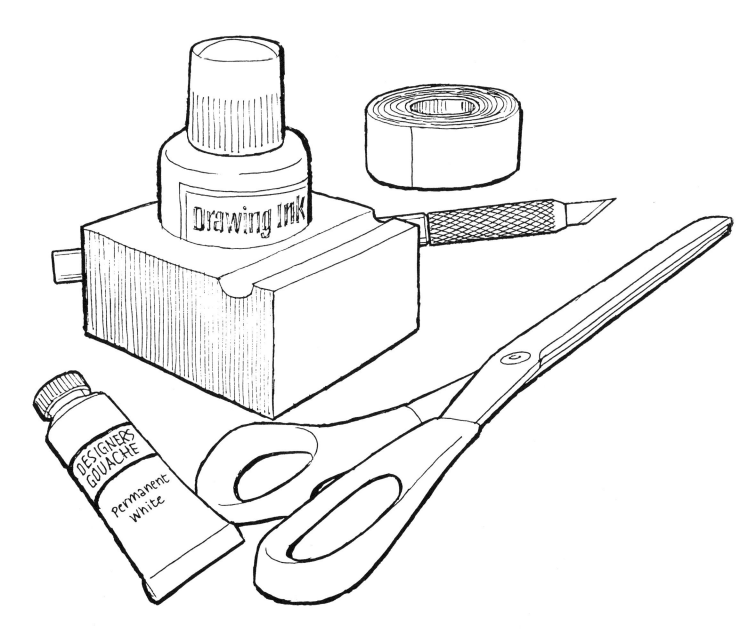

Broad-edged pen strokes

Whether cut from reeds or quills the broad-edged pen was the major letter-making tool until the invention of printing, its characteristic thick and thin strokes surviving in many typographic letters. A modern equivalent of these pens is the broad-edged fibre-tipped pen which is available in various widths, and this kind of pen is used in this demonstration and for the majority of the examples in this book.

Writing is best done on a sloping surface of about 10 degrees and when held as shown below the pen's angle to the writing surface will be approximately 60 degrees. It is best to find the position on the writing surface where the writing feels easiest (or least difficult) and to move the paper along as the writing progresses, keeping the hand in the same position throughout.

Because the writing arm is connected to a shoulder and does not grow directly out of the middle of the chest it is natural that the pen will be at an angle to the writing line, as shown in position (1) below. This tilt of the pen's edge – approximately 30 degrees – results in the typical vertical, horizontal, diagonal and curved strokes shown here. Notice that the widest stroke is the top left to bottom right

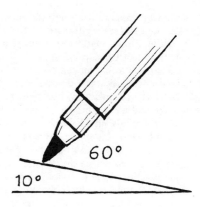

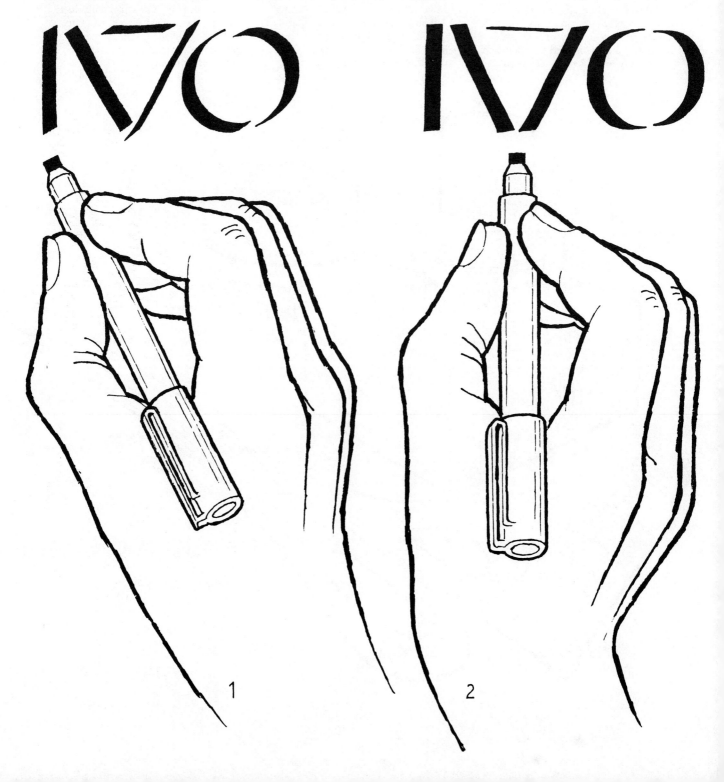

1

2

diagonal while the top right to bottom left diagonal and the horizontal are thinnest. The curves have a pronounced tilt or stress, swelling from thin to thick and back to thin. Several other strokes resulting from this pen angle are shown at (1a).

It is possible to ignore the natural angle described above and pull the pen round so that its edge is parallel to the writing line, as in (2), to produce a full width vertical, matching diagonals, a very thin horizontal and curves without any tilt. Other strokes are shown at (2a). This rather difficult to maintain

writing angle is rarely used but can be seen in some kinds of uncial letter (see page 26).

The very rare pen position shown at (3) is here mainly for demonstration purposes. In this case the opposite of position (2) occurs, with a very thin vertical, wide horizontal, matching half-width diagonals and curves weighted at top and bottom and thin at the sides. Other strokes resulting from this eccentric pen angle are shown at (3a). They are suggestive of some oriental scripts that employ a great variety of pen angles.

1a

2a

3a

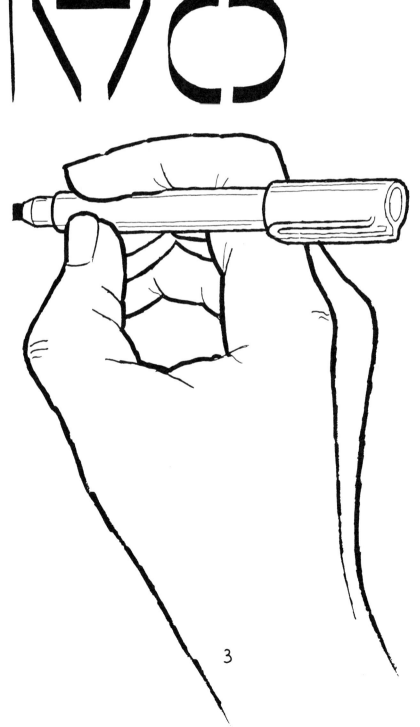

3

Flexible pointed pen and brush strokes

The important difference between the writing tools described here and the broad-edged pen is that, whereas the edged pen produces thick and thin strokes that vary according to the angle and direction of movement, flexible pens and brushes require pressure to make thicker lines. Increasing pressure brings thicker lines as the nib opens or the brush's bristles spread to release a wider flow of ink. The illustration below (1) shows this happening with a steel nib and above some typical vertical, horizontal, diagonal and curved strokes.

A recently introduced pointed instrument which has the feel of a brush with some of a pen's rigidity is the Mars Graphic 3000 pen. If this is held vertically above the writing sur-

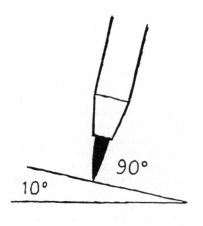

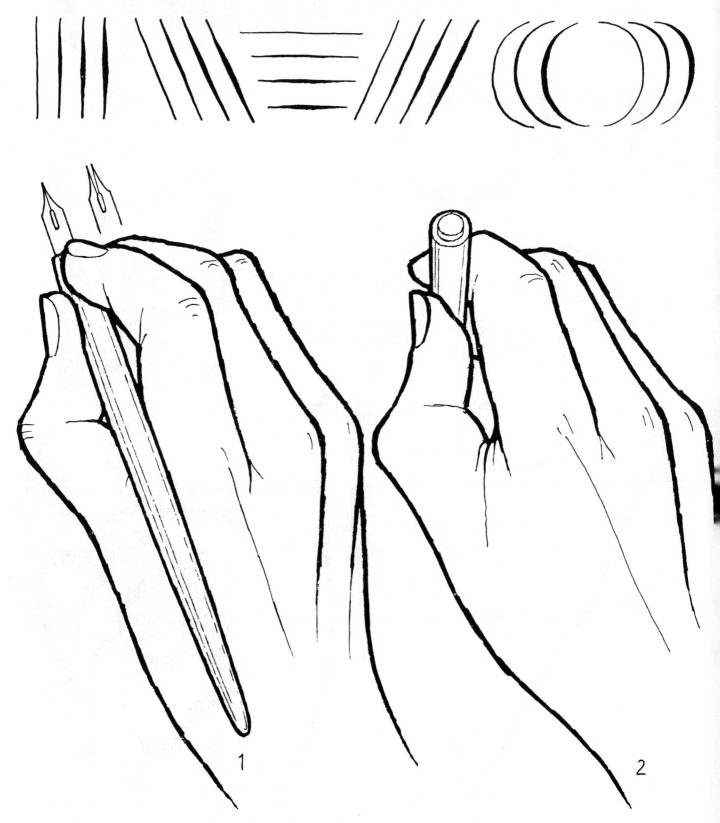

1

2

face, as shown left and at (2) below, the marks it makes will be similar to those of a pointed pen but requiring less pressure. Further examples of both tools' stroke-making are shown at (1a) and (2a). Typical pointed pen scripts are the copperplate styles described on page 38).

Pointed brushes respond to changes in writing pressure to a far greater degree than the steel nib. Both pressure and angle can be altered so that even quite a thin brush produces very wide strokes as its bristles are worked on their side. The variety of marks that a brush can make are infinite – a few are shown at (3a) – and many brush scripts have been developed for their flavour of informality and as a contrast to the more rigid typographic letter.

1a

2a

3

3a

The geometric basis of capital letters is well demonstrated in Paul Renner's Futura, shown right, and in the diagram below. This sanserif, monoline letter uses classic roman proportions – some letters wide, some narrow – and is a good model for writing practice with a pointed fibre-tipped pen. The stroke-making sequence is shown in the alphabet below, with alternative forms for some characters. Although it may seem easier to make letters *C*, *O* and *S* in one stroke the sequence shown will give more control over their forms.

ABCDEFGHIJK
LMNOPQRST
UVWXYZ

Typeface: Futura

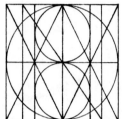

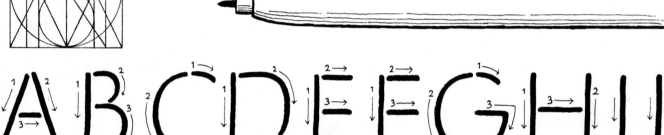

Use fine fibre-tipped pens or Rotring technical pens to make smaller letters, simplifying the stroke-making sequence to suit the small scale where this seems necessary. This will develop skill in type indication on layouts and visuals and although not writing as generally understood it will instil a habit of consistent stroke-making that is essential in calligraphy.

DESIGNER
BOOKJACKET CHAPTER HEADING
LETTER SPACING TYPOGRAPHIC SPECIFICATION

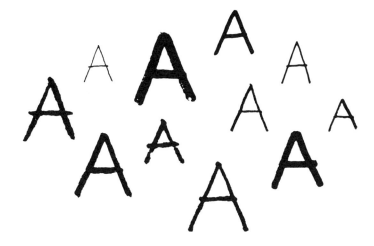

Even when using such plain letters as these capitals some variety in line thickness and expressive quality can be achieved by using different pens and papers. Use pointed rather than broad-edged pens and notice that where the ink bleeds into an absorbent paper an attractive, rough-edged line may result. The group of letters shown left vary both in size and line quality. For more about papers see page 50.

The rendering of the groups of words below shows the changes in weight achieved by writing with pens of an increasing thickness, while compressing the letter proportions produces yet another variation.

THE OTHER SIDE OF THE TRACK   THE OTHER SIDE OF THE TRACK   **THE OTHER SIDE OF THE TRACK**

THE OTHER SIDE OF THE TRACK

GRAPHIC
GRAPHIC
GRAPHIC

The American calligrapher Lloyd Reynolds observed that in lettering the eye is conservative, wanting to recognise the forms with which it is familiar, while the hand is innovative, impatient of formality, and tries to take short cuts as it guides the pen. This tension between eye and hand is evident as the writing speed increases. Letters begin to lose their separateness, to join and to incline in the direction of the writing, the lively cursive quality that results being achieved at the expense of the original forms. Writing speed has been one of the influences through which letterforms evolved up until the time of the invention of printing types. Once familiar with these simple capitals it is enjoyable to practise writing them with increasing freedom, as shown left.

The usual variations in stroke width in roman capitals are clearly shown in Hermann Zapf's elegant typeface Optima, whose proportions are similar to Futura. The written forms that underlie this letter can be reconstructed with a broad-edged pen approximately one-tenth the height of the letter held at a shallow angle, following the sequence shown in the alphabet below. To achieve the thin verticals in *M* and *N* the broad edge should be twisted to 60 degrees. It will be seen that the strokes produced lack the slight waisting of the typographic letters, a subtle effect that can be obtained by pressure variations when writing with steel nibs or quill pens, or with the rigid fibre-tipped pen by twisting its broad edge from 0 to 30 degrees and back to 0 degrees as it travels down a vertical stem, as shown in detail (c) below.

Optima lacks the usual serifs of roman capitals and four ways of adding serifs to these written letters are shown in the enlarged details below. Detail (a)

Typeface: Optima

is the simplest kind of serif, a rounded lead-in stroke to the left of the vertical and a lead-out stroke to the right. An alternative serif made by the pen travelling horizontally before moving down the vertical is also shown. Detail (b) shows another simple serif made by a horizontal pen stroke ending vertical stems. At endings to horizontal strokes a slight twisting of the pen to a steeper angle will give a thickening at the end with a short hairline to finish, or the pen may be turned onto one corner and pulled down to produce a curved hairline. Detail (c) shows the pen manipulation already described above, with the changes in angle producing curved serifs as the broad edge is

twisted into a vertical position at the end of horizontal strokes, and vertical strokes being completed with horizontal hairlines made by the pen on its thinnest edge. Detail (d) shows the serif achieved by the broad edge held horizontally and pulled down in a curve into the vertical and leaving in another curve on the baseline, returning to complete the horizontals and add an extra balancing curve at both ends to overlap and blend with the vertical. When used in conjunction with the waisted strokes shown in (c) this method produces the most sophisticated letterforms, but these techniques require great skill. In type design these qualities are achieved by drawing

rather than writing the letters, giving the designer absolute control over their forms.

The choice of ratio between width of pen and height of letter is quite wide, and the extremes of lightness and boldness that can be obtained by varying the stroke width for letters of the same height is shown right. As thickness of stroke increases some proportions alter to accommodate the extra weight and blackness.

ITS ALL A QUESTION OF WHAT YOU WANT

ITS ALL A QUESTION OF WHAT YOU WANT

RHYTHM-MAKERS

COMPRESSION

Unlike type the written letter can be given great freedom in alignment and certain strokes, such as the tails of *R*, *K* and *Y*, can be extended for expressive effect, as shown above.

Pen-written capitals may be condensed to give taller letters in a given space, but *M* and *N* must not be allowed to become too heavy. Turning the pen further to an angle of 60 degrees produces a letter that has thinner verticals and is easier to compress. The resulting changes in stress and the thicker horizontals are reminiscent of rustic roman capitals of the fifth century.

COMPRESSION

Uncials

Round forms predominate in this book script that evolved from capital letters in the fifth century and includes ascending and descending strokes. This typeface, similar to Hammer Uncial, (they were both designed by Victor Hammer) imitates writing produced with a horizontally held broad-edged pen and the typical forms with strong junctions between curves and verticals are made clear in the diagram below. An angled pen can also be used to write uncial letters, as shown in the alphabet below, to give a pronounced stress to the curves and a lightening of some junctions.

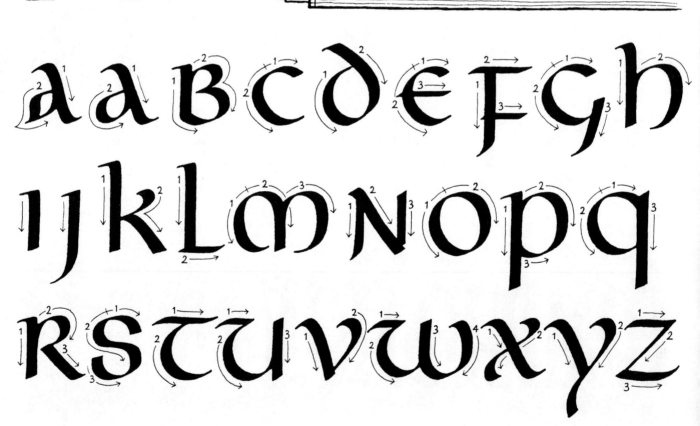

Typeface: American Uncial

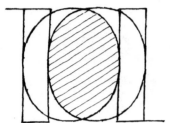

Serifs can be added to the beginnings of vertical strokes with an extra diagonal mark filling the space between the vertical and the lead-in hairline. For horizontal strokes the pen should be twisted as it travels from left to right, beginning or ending at 90 degrees depending on whether the serif begins or finishes the stroke.

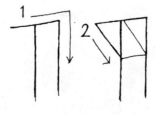
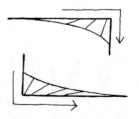

Half-uncials

Like the uncial, the *half-uncial* letter is a transitional form and closely linked with the spread of Christianity and the writing of ecclesiastical manuscripts. Several minuscule letters such as *e*, *f*, *m* and *r* are already fully developed in these letters, while *g* is still in an intermediate form. The grandeur of uncial letters and the more fluid quality of half-uncials are seen in the two examples below, *Anglo-Saxon* using a more familiar form of *g*.

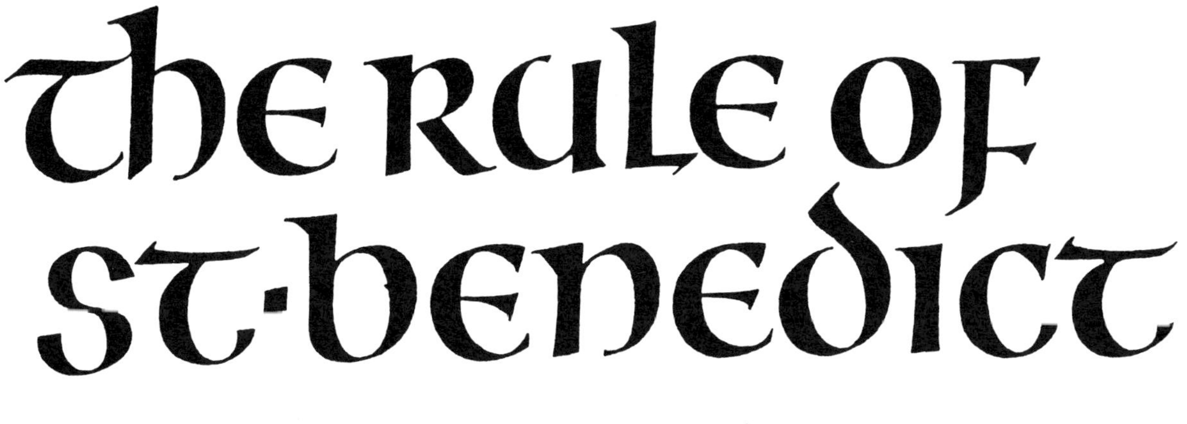

abdefgk
lmnrxy

the rule of
st·benedict

Anglo·Saxon

Because of its strong associations with early Christian art and its archaic flavour uncial has few uses today, but its unusual and unconventional forms can be the basis for creative experiment. A title of compressed, closely grouped uncials, below, and a monoline design that mixes uncial with half-uncial letters, below right, illustrate two possible graphic approaches.

the
making of
letters

the
making
of
letters

Minuscules

The *minuscule* script of the ninth century, which evolved from earlier styles including uncials, later became the model for the first roman printing types in the fifteenth century. This twentieth-century example of a lowercase roman type is Bruce Rogers' Centaur. The basic structure and the broad-edged pen's simple stroke-making sequence in this minuscule script is shown in the diagram and alphabet below. Pen angle is 30 degrees and the main body of the letters is five pen widths high, with ascenders and descenders extending for approximately three-quarters of the body height. Double foot serifs can follow the styles described on page 24, and the angled serifs for some verticals are shown at the foot of this page.

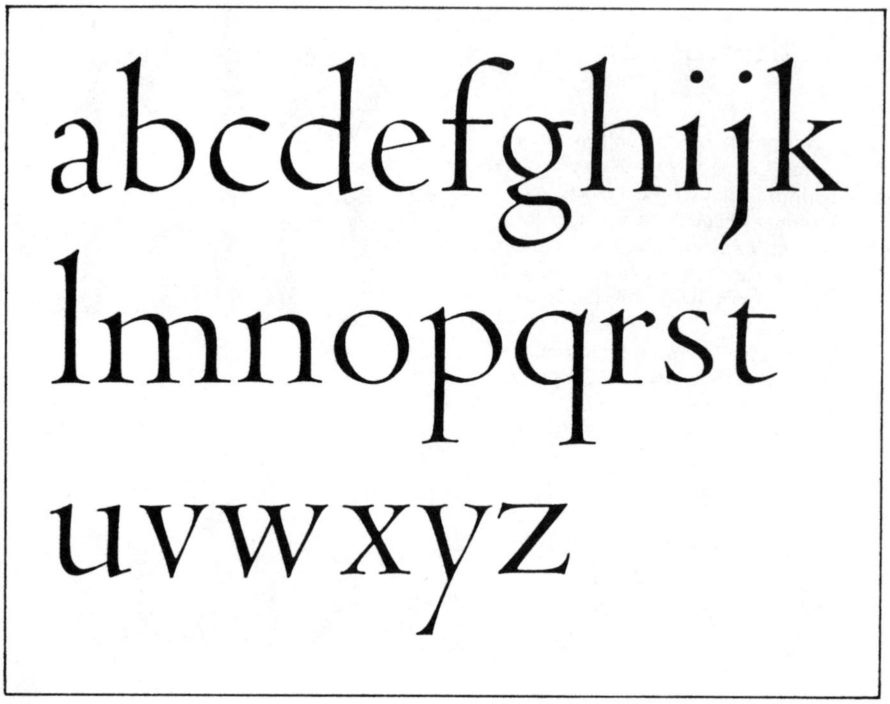

abcdefghijk
lmnopqrst
uvwxyz

Typeface: Centaur

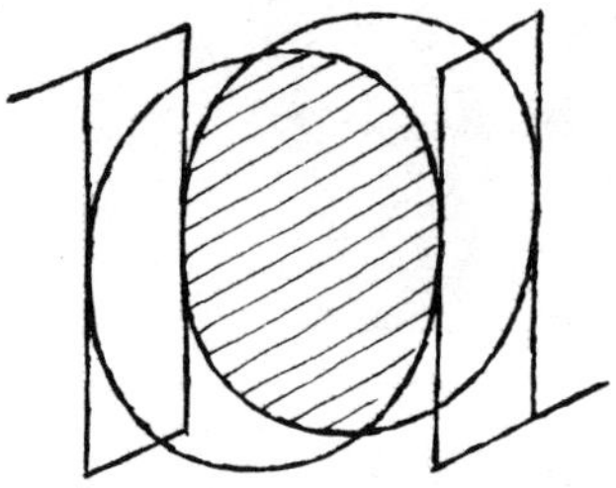

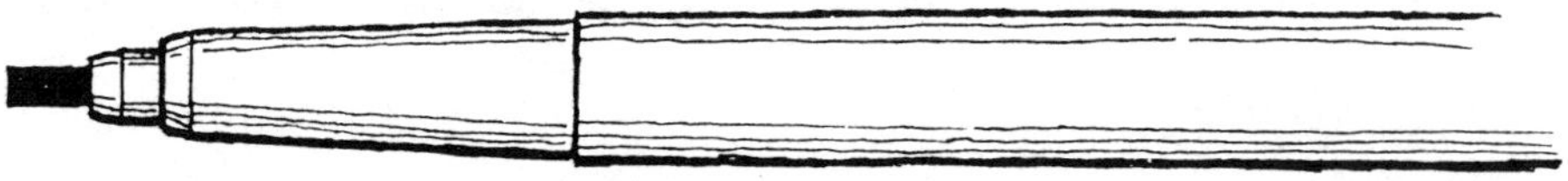

The Alphabet ²⁹

Prospectus

Capital initial letters should be shorter than the height of ascending strokes and the treatment of serifs in both alphabets should be consistent.

As with other scripts already described the ratio of pen width to letter height can be varied considerably, as in the two examples shown right. Single serifs in both these examples give the lettering greater liveliness than in the formal rendering above.

twenty six

Arabic numerals first appeared in a European manuscript in the tenth century and are shown here in the non-ranging style that matches minuscule letters.

1234567890

The effect of compressing letters whose basic structure is circular has already been seen in this book (see pages 23, 25, 27) and here this gives the pattern of these minuscule forms a strong vertical bias with an increase in weight – a preview of the more angular styles to come.

Scriptorium

Blackletter

The complex group of Gothic scripts known as *blackletter* is commonly thought to be embodied in the kind of typeface shown here, Old English, but this is only one style, *textura*, amid several, of which three others, *fraktur*, *schwabacher* and *rotunda* will also be described in these pages. These scripts evolved during the period 1300–1500, developing gradually from the preceding minuscule letter to the most extremely compressed and angular form called textura. The first printing type, cast in Mainz in the mid-fifteenth century by Johann Gutenberg, was based on textura script. Although immensely powerful and decorative, compared with the simplicity and naturalness of uncial and minuscule scripts, blackletter characters are highly contrived, artificial and relatively illegible. In the English-speaking world blackletter can today appear anachronistic or medieval, but in German-speaking cultures it has survived in everyday use and their lettering is the richer for it.

It can be difficult to use blackletter in contemporary graphics – its medieval associations can be overwhelming – but if kept simple and free from elaborate detail these letters offer the designer a powerful alternative to roman scripts, and may be a basis for further experiment. Capital letters for use with these scripts are shown on pages 32–33.

Typeface: Old English

In the four blackletter styles shown here the differences between each alphabet have been emphasised to an extent that is not always evident in historical examples. Serifs and decorative details have been severely curtailed for the sake of clarity, and the reader should find the stroke-making sequence in each alphabet easy to work out. Pen angle varies from 30 to 45 degrees and the 45 degree foot serif and the double serifs that may end some ascenders and descenders are shown right.

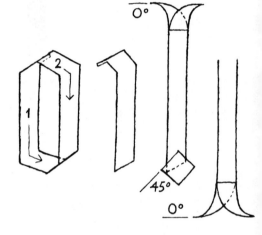

Textura

This style is almost devoid of curves, being made up mostly from short, straight strokes meeting at angles. It is a very narrow letter in which the blackness of the pen strokes emphasises the white spaces inside and between the letters. Ascenders and descenders are short – minimal line spacing increases the textural pattern – and may end in double serifs.

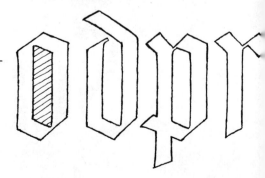

abcdefghijklmn
opqrstuvwxyz

Fraktur

The appearance of this script is less angular than textura because of the presence of some curved strokes and the softer treatment of some details. In contrast with the curves the straight strokes meeting at angles look fractured or broken – hence the name *fraktur*.

abcdefghijklmn
opqrstuvwxyz

Schwabacher

A predominance of curved strokes makes this the least severe of these blackletter styles. The pointed *o* and *e* are very characteristic.

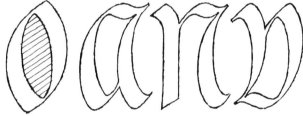

abcdefghijklmn
opqrstuvwxyz

Rotunda

This letter flourished in southern Europe, especially in Italy and Spain. As its name implies it is a rounder, wider character than the other styles depicted here, having more affinity with minuscule letters (see page 28). The two-storey *a* is similar.

32 **Capitals**

Gothic capital letters used as initials were often very complex and illegible, so today simpler forms are better. The early practice that based capitals on uncial forms (see page 26) may be followed, as shown in this alphabet (right) which uses a 30 degree pen angle. Below a variant using some typically Gothic capitals that include many curved strokes is shown, and ways in which further embellishment may be added with extra strokes are suggested in the margins. The degree to which the designer embellishes these capitals is partly a matter of taste, but good historical examples should be studied too (see Bibliography, page 221).

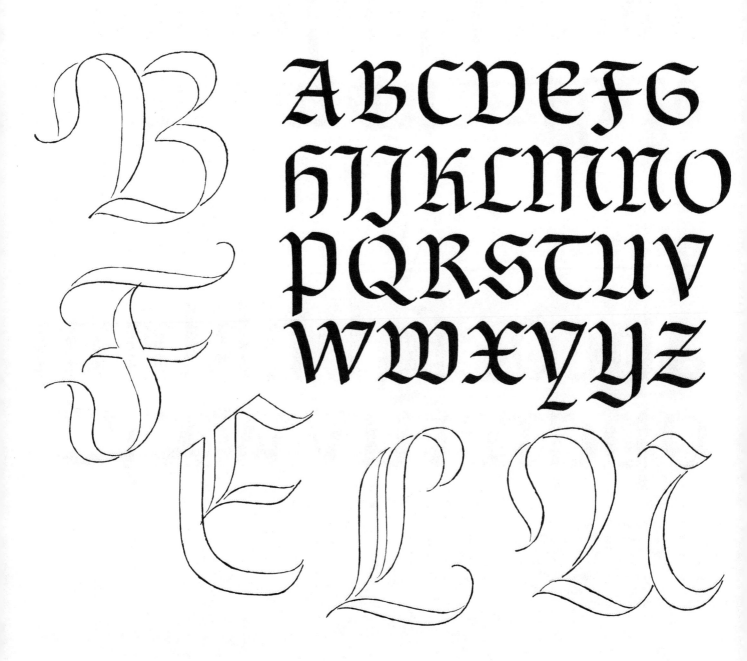

ABCDEFG
HIJKLMN
OPQRSTU
VWXYZ

An alternative to uncial-based capitals is the pen-written roman capital alphabet shown left. There are distinctive junctions in some letters that provide a stylistic link with blackletter scripts, as does the angular *K*. A horizontal stroke across the top of *A* – as in the alphabet opposite – would add a further authentic touch.

Very simple, almost sanserif roman capitals, which contrast strongly with the calligraphic text style, can be very effective. The alphabet shown below, which uses a horizontal stroke on *J* and leaves the middle horizontal of *B* unconnected to match *P* and *R*, has been given extra strength by overlapping the pen strokes to make shapely wedge-shaped stroke endings. The pen angle must vary considerably to achieve this effect, which is shown in detail in the margins.

ABCDEFG
HIJKLMN
OPQRSTU
VWXYZ

Changes in line, form and weight

Changes in line, form and weight

Changes in line, form and weight

the Piano player

Blackletter has been much neglected in the graphic arts or used only in a narrow hackneyed way to suggest the middle ages or the antique. Some of the power, beauty and graphic potential of blackletter is evident in the examples on this and the opposite page.

Reducing the ratio between pen width and letter height results in a progressively blacker appearance to the groups of textura shown at the top of this page, the powerful pattern of the blackest example greatly reducing legibility – but high legibility is not always the purpose of lettering. The initial stands clear of the script to avoid disturbing the vertical pattern.

Increasing the height of textura letters gives them an even stronger vertical emphasis, as shown above. A double stroke initial provides a contrast of curves in this line of angular letters.

In the group on the right the straights and curves of fraktur are seen against plain bold capitals.

Myths & Sagas of Northern Europe

Vivaldi
Albinoni
Corelli

Decorative initial letters, and the curves of schwabacher lend a suitable musical flavour to the names of three baroque composers, above.

Below, rotunda letters are used in two sizes for this very apt quotation from George Bernard Shaw.

The Tenth Man

Zodiac

Fanfare

The examples above show three graphic treatments of written letters, including the use of outline drawing and a screen tint to reduce visual weight.

The golden rule
is that there are no golden rules

Narrow letters at a modest slope characterise the *italic* script of the fifteenth century on which the typeface Bembo is based. In its written form the pen angle is close to 35 degrees and the letters are slightly sloped at about 5 degrees, as shown in the diagram below, while the alphabet shows the stroke sequence as well as alternative characters and stroke endings. The compressed oval of the *o* is echoed in several letters and thin upswept diagonals and steeply angled serifs contribute to the cursive effect.

abcdefghijk
lmnopqrstu
vwxyz

Typeface: Bembo

Serifs may be made in a tight curve at start and finish of strokes, or given an acute sharpness (far right).

Initial capitals may be upright romans, kept quite short (right) or sloped to match the script (below) while the lower example uses a swash on the initial *B*. The three examples here also show different pen width to letter height ratios, and the word *Bibliophile* uses the alternative forms of ascender and descender shown on the previous page, varying the ascender heights to avoid monotony. Slight variations in letter slope will also avoid a monotonous regularity in italic, particularly where several lines of writing occur.

Fine &
Dandy

Alternative
Bibliophile

Ampersands are a space-saving and decorative device and several varieties may be used with italic scripts, choice depending on the kind of effect desired.

& & & & & &

The already narrow forms of italic can be further compressed, steepening the thin diagonals (right) or lifting the pen to make a higher junction (far right). Very compressed letters look best with a minimum slope, and may even be upright.

The informality of handwriting with many letters joining is suggested in the cursive script below.

snap neo

The Chairman's secretary

38 Copperplate

This group of scripts, that flourished from 1600–1800, were written with flexible pens (see page 20) or engraved on copper printing plates. The typeface Youthline Script is one of many to imitate the style of *copperplate* writing, having a slope of 40 degrees. The basic forms of the style are shown in the diagram below, with an alphabet of unstressed letters and several characters written with the pressure variations that produce a thickening of some strokes and curves. Much practice is needed to maintain regularity of slope and rhythmical pen pressure. Guidelines and the letter slope indicated in pencil are essential, and it is also helpful to turn the paper away from the horizontal.

Typeface: Youthline Script (capitals opposite)

The pointed brush, which responds to the slightest pressure, is able to render a copperplate style in several weights and degrees of refinement, and may be used forcefully to produce bold and informal letters. The Mars 3000 pen makes lines of both delicacy and softness while remaining flexible enough to produce bold swelling lines under pressure.

A B C D E F G H I
J K L M N O P Q R
S T U V W X Y Z

Capital letters in the copperplate style are reserved for initials – like blackletter initials they are too complex to be used together – and are formed by similar writing movements and pressure variations as in the script. Historically they were often considerably taller than the script letter, as shown right, but today they may be shortened (below).

Penman

Penman

Some alternative serifs and stroke endings are shown right. The curved hairline serif is sometimes replaced by a plain horizontal cut-off, which may be slightly concave on the baseline to avoid a flat-footed appearance. A more natural sloped ending to the start and finish of downstrokes is shown far right, together with the typical endings that arise from ink build-up at the ends of fine curves. These are seen in the words below which, like most copperplate used in the graphic arts, have been drawn to simulate the script letter.

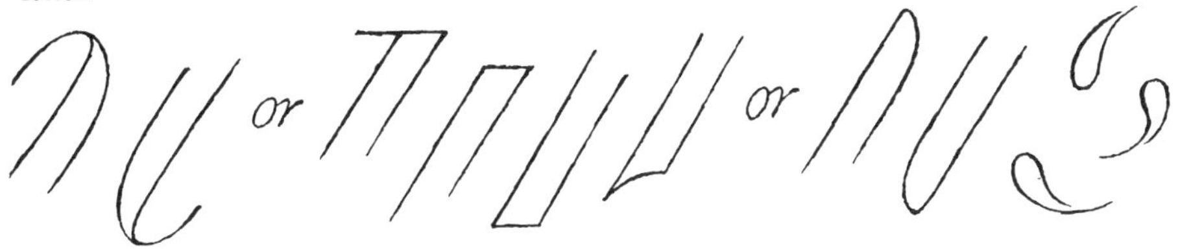

Birth and Education

menu

While writing with the pointed brush employs similar manipulation of pressure as pen-written copperplate script, the visual results can be very different, as shown in *menu*, where the brush has been used at an angle to obtain the widest possible downstrokes and sharply angled endings.

As an exuberant extension to some letters the flourish has long been used to enhance writing, often attaining great intricacy of pattern, especially in the eighteenth and nineteenth centuries. The broad-edged pen flourishes (right) show a constant pen angle of about 30 degrees, while below are some typical *swash* letters including two examples (*h* and *d*) of contrived flourishes that seriously detract from the legibility of these letters. In the word below the swash on the middle *e* breaks the word in two – this character is best used at the end of a line. Lyn Gathercole's bookplate uses a long back-swept flourish to balance the lettering and fill the space beneath. In the sequence below right the unadorned word is progressively dressed up in flourishes, the final version's lower flourish extending from the capital because the other letters are not capable of downward extension. Whether this fifth state is better than the others is a matter of taste.

The flourishes (right) are not broad-edged pen based but derive from copperplate engraving practice, the lines swelling and thinning freely to suit the decorative effect. In the title below the surrounding flourishes, which do not connect with the words, have been drawn with the aid of French curves and a technical pen (see detail).

Flourishing is a difficult art to master, especially today when it can easily look anachronistic or like fancy dress. Restraint is normally the best policy. It is worth studying the work of the few contemporary masters, such as Reynolds Stone, Leo Wyatt (both engravers), Jean Larcher and Claude Mediavilla for examples of flourishing handled with assurance and taste.

Experimenting with non-calligraphic pens and brushes or even non-pens can produce exciting and unpredictable results.

Balsa wood

Soft and very absorbent strips of balsa wood make good pens for large writing but need to be dipped into the ink frequently. Cut the wood at an angle to suit your hand. The alphabet shown here is suitable for writing with balsa wood following the varying pen angle sequence shown in the diagram. This letter is reminiscent of Rudolf Koch's Neuland typeface.

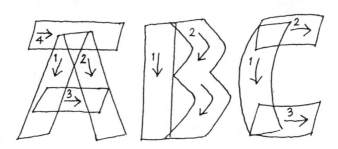

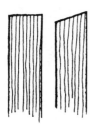

The rapid ink loss and frequent re-loading of a balsa wood pen can lead to considerable variations in tone, especially when the ink is non-waterproof as in this example (right).

If the wood's edge is broken unevenly cruder letters result, as in the line above, while the group on the right shows that each letter *a* is different, depending on the amount of ink the wood retains.

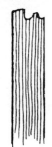

Ruling pen

The draughtsman's ruling pen, with its screw adjustment to control line width, can produce writing of great vigour, as these examples show. Varying the angle of the pen controls ink flow; the shallower the angle the greater the flow. Speedy execution is necessary to prevent flooding. The German letterer Fritz Poppl was largely responsible for developing this technique.

Round brush

The freely formed letter shown here was swiftly written with a large soft round-ended brush held vertically over the paper, its shape first sketched several times in the air above the surface of the paper. Spontaneous letters made in this way have an accidental quality that is far removed from conventional broad-edged pen forms.

In this technique a pen of narrower width than the bold strokes is used to build up the letters progressively, as shown opposite and on page 33. Although slower than writing this drawing method gives great control over the forms, and if done with short strokes the overlap can give an attractively irregular edge. With larger letters white can be allowed to appear between strokes to further enliven the effect. Other possibilities include leaving white space between the pen strokes to make an outline letter, using pens of different widths and repeating strokes to achieve a multiple line image. This last effect can also be produced in single strokes with special multiple-edged pens.

Graphic techniques

The following pages describe some of
the methods by which the written letter
can be modified or developed for
graphic purposes.

Re-touching

It is usually necessary to strengthen
serifs and hairlines when working for
reproduction, principally to allow for
the thinning effects of photo-reduction,
and desirable to remove irregularities
that may seem out of place in print.
Re-touching with a technical pen and
white gouache also extends the letterer's control over the forms, enabling
him to get *exactly* what he wants. In the
example shown here the original was
written at a comfortable size and the
initial added afterwards, then on an
enlarged photocopy the junctions were
strengthened and serifs given a crisp-
ness they lacked in the original. It is
important not to over re-touch or the
calligraphic character may be lost.
Finally the lettering was reduced to its
reproduction size. For further reduction all the letters were again strengthened so that they would not appear
too thin in small sizes.

In the example below pen-drawn letters are the basis for the highly
finished, visually edited characters of a
typeface. The display of four names
clearly shows that the discipline of type
design has not removed the letter's calligraphic appearance.

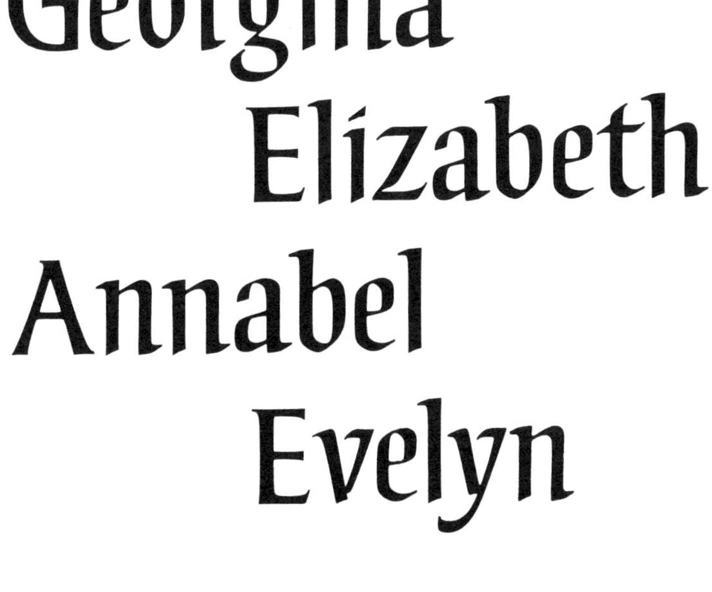

Maestro

Maes

Maestro

Maestro

Maestro

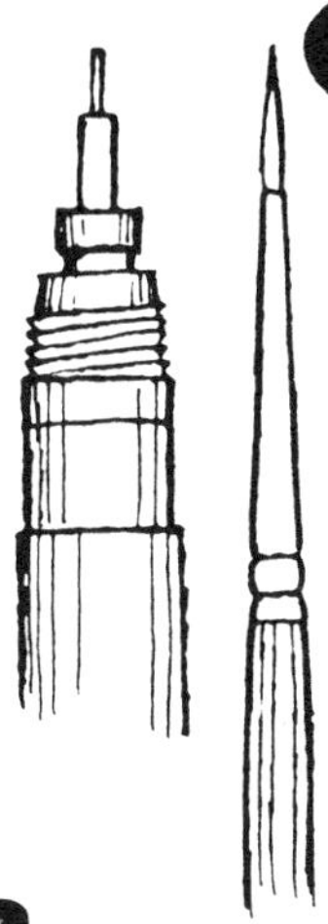

Georgina

Elizabeth

Annabel

Evelyn

abc

abc

Cut and paste

Because of the control that can be exercised when working for reproduction even the most apparently spontaneous line of writing can be faked to achieve the desired result. In the headline shown here several exploratory lines were first written to assess the general effect and particularly the style of the capital letters and the treatment of their horizontal strokes. The final version was assembled from several pieces of writing, the best parts of each cut out and pasted down to make up the complete headline. This can be retouched if necessary before a photocopy is made to obliterate all evidence of the sleight-of-hand that produced this apparently freely written line of script.

Enlargements

Using a photocopier that enlarges the image makes it simple to take a piece of writing made at a convenient size and enlarge it through several stages to achieve a dramatic increase in both size and power. If the original has a textured quality or a rough edge those features will be that much more expressive.

48

Calligraphy

calligraphy

calligraphy

Careful visual editing and re-touching have improved the junctions and other details in this very informal continuous brush script. The original, shown far left, has been greatly enlarged on a photocopier and the editing done on that image. Most junctions have bene- fited from the insertion of more white space, the initial letter has been streng- thened, the space between p and h (the only break in this word) has been increased slightly and the tail of y given a more emphatic termination.

Following this refining process an outline drawing was made of the enlarged image and on a photocopy of that the background filled in with a black marker to provide a reversed image. In the final reduction back to the original size the positive, outline and negative versions retain the informal vitality of the original writing with additional clarity – a further exam- ple of the extra control over letters afforded by sensitive re-touching.

The writing surface should provide enough resistance to the writing instrument to allow good pen control, but if rougher surfaces are used, such as watercolour paper, a degree of texture will result as depressions in the white paper show through the pen strokes. This effect can be increased if the pen is running dry, as shown in *Zulu*. The example below was written with a pointed fibre-tipped pen on blotting paper, while the highly absorbent surface of a paper towel which sucked most of the ink out of the brush on first impact produced the examples (lower right) giving a top heavy appearance to *North*. Exciting effects can be obtained when unusual writing materials lessen the designer's control over letterforms, and experiment can result in useful discoveries.

A resist prevents ink or paint adhering
to the writing surface. In the example
(left) the letters were written in rubber
cement with a strip of balsa wood.
When dry a coat of ink was applied
and allowed to dry thoroughly before
rubbing with an eraser to remove all
the rubber cement revealing the white
lettering. A crayon pencil provided the
resist on a strongly textured paper
(below).

Rubbings

Rubbings may be done with the side of
a soft pencil point to pick up the
paper's texture. In the example (above
left) letters were cut from Canson
paper (two layers glued together to give
greater thickness) and mounted on
card with the counter of *O* carefully
repositioned. After the rubbing was
completed traces of pencil on the letters were removed with white paint.
The example left shows the effect
achieved with raised letters cut from
thick, coarse-surfaced paper. Here the
rubbing picks up the background to
provide further interest.

Masks

In this extension of the resist principal
letters cut from paper (in this example
those removed from the first rubbing
described above) were fixed to card
with rubber cement. Ink or paint may
be sprayed on or, as in this case, stip-
pled with a soft brush to cover both
letters and background. When the
paper letters were removed the resulting soft-edged forms were bolder than
the original paper letters.

52   **Stencils**

A stencil allows a piece of writing to be repeated, perhaps to build up a pattern, and provides great scope in the use of colour. The natural breaks in pen-written letters make a good basis for stencil cutting, providing the necessary links that maintain the stencil's structure. The words in this example were first written with a broad-edged pen then a tracing was transferred to card and the stencil cut with a craft knife. Acrylic paint is an excellent medium for stencilling because its thick consistency prevents it from spreading under the stencil. Here it has been applied with a stiff stencil brush using vertical dabbing movements, but other kinds of brush can be tried to obtain different effects. The resulting letters have a pleasingly irregular edge, and the paint-spattered stencil provides a further image.

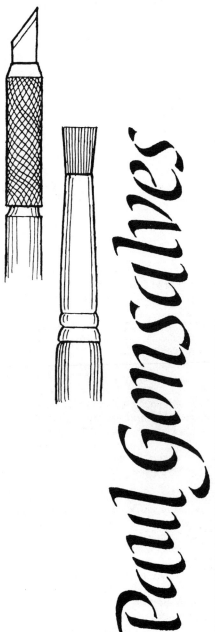

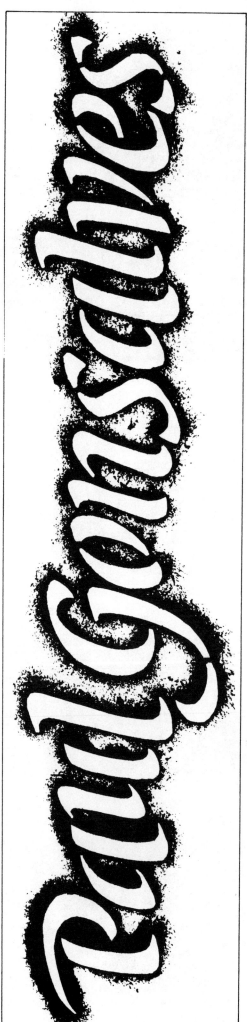

Multiple images

Repeating a word to build up a pattern is a graphic cliché, but livelier ideas are shown here with the repetition of a word in varying sizes (obtained with a photocopier) to make a visually expressive image, enhanced by stippling with white gouache. Below overlapping and repetition build up a dense but powerful design. This latter example, which employed pens of various widths, sacrifices legibility for expression and therefore belongs outside the usual area of day-to-day graphic communication.

The written letter's advantage over type lies in its flexibility, its liveliness and visual richness. These attributes can be used to great effect in monograms, logotypes and titles, with longer texts best left to type. Several examples are shown here and in the following pages.

Broad-edged pen

The illustrations on this page and pages 55–57 were made with broad-edged pens, the design opposite showing contrasts in style and weight with bold minuscules and light capitals, while even stronger contrast marks the *FG* monogram with bold, chunky letters – the result of much pen twisting – underlined by a line of small, light capitals. The initial *A* uses texture and open-ended double strokes, and the double *GG* design makes an impact by twisting the letters through 45 degrees to match the pen angle.

In this title (left) a large initial is used but the main effect is in the diagonals of the three *Y*s. The uncial *E* increases the number of round letters in this all capital design, and a discreet joining of *N* with *F* is not allowed to become intrusive. Set close together the lines make a strong but legible letter pattern.

Both *Fourteen* and *Centaur* use condensed capitals with irregular alignment. In the first example the curved letters are squared considerably to marry with the straight characters, the long, angled serifs and rough edges contributing to its graphic energy. *Centaur* uses light, curvy capitals in a sweeping linear pattern.

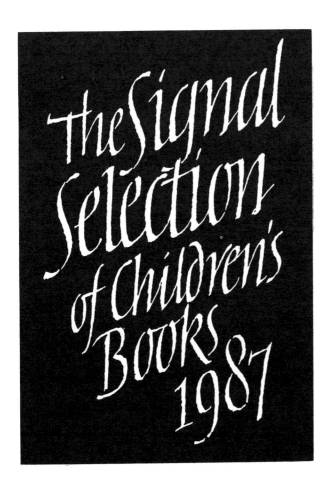

Pen-written characters can easily be overlapped to increase a design's homogeneity as shown above where contrast in size and weight add to the drama. The design's unity is increased by horizontal ligatures linking the light to the bold letters.

In this cover design (left) an informal script has been written on a slope, the usually inclined characters' now upright stance adds to the energy of the design and reversing the writing white out of a black ground increases impact considerably.

SHONAGON

THE Warriors OF Tusani

Stacking letters vertically is usually regarded as a bad practice but here where they are all symmetrical and the intention is to echo Chinese writing the effect is pleasing, with letters that have a brushy quality.

The monogram (below left) required several changes in pen angle to achieve its rather oriental flavour, and its softly tinted rendering is given a sharper definition by the irregularly drawn outline – another example of the value of contrast in even the simplest of designs.

In the title at the top of this page very compressed angular italic is aggressive and war-like. The vigorous rendering heightens this effect. Below, the ruled horizontal lines provide both a setting for and a contrast to a freely written script, while the white space inside *Review* flows between the characters and into the surrounding area giving an elegant, fluid quality. The thicker strokes add an apparent depth to this design.

Personal Statement

REVIEW

In this title (left) capital letters of different heights make three almost equal length lines (if exactly equal the effect might have been too formal). The uncommon form of *Y*, swash *P* and open-bowled *R*s give this design its individuality.

The title below, whose rolling movement and stretched out appearance perhaps reflect the subject, was written quite lightly with the pen angled and twisted so that its contact with the rough paper varied from the full width to merely a corner of its edge.

In the line above a distinctive movement is created by giving uncial letters a cursive slope more usual in italic, the pen's angle varying from near horizontal to about 20 degrees. This is an example of a creative contemporary development of an historic letterform.

When combining letters into a monogram it is often enough to look for similarities that can be exploited, as in *av* where the choice of the sloped uncial *a* provides an almost reversed mirror image of *v*. Strong diagonals and the close-fitting background shape which emphasises the spaces in and around the letters make this a distinctive yet simple design.

Brush and pointed pen

The illustrations on this and the following two pages were done with a variety of brushes and pointed pens, the first three examples on this page with the same number 2 brush. In the title shown right considerable variations in finger pressure were required to achieve the strong contrast in the built-up strokes, the almost vertical letters having similarities to eighteenth-century typefaces such as Bodoni and Didot. To achieve the fine entry and exit strokes the brush was held upright, as was the case in the line of script below, a freely written version of copperplate. Some preliminary pencil sketching helped to guide the brush and resting the writing hand on the other hand facilitated the sweeping brush movements in this large-scale script. Re-touching produced the final polish.

Showing a greater slope than the examples above, this title (right) was also written with greater speed with most letters being connected. The brush was held as in everyday writing, with the pressure variations less marked than in the previous examples.

The aggressive design *aggro* was made on rough paper with a blunt stencil brush held upright and dipped frequently in black gouache. Notice how in such bold lettering the white spaces become positive shapes.

Pennies from heaven

Virtuoso

Post Card Collection

The great flexibility of the pointed brush is evident in this monogram, the stroke starting at the inner point and spiralling out with increasing pressure to produce the background shape that defines letter *C*. The original was made at approximately one-third of the size shown here.

Beast has a scratchy appearance that resulted from attacking the writing surface in quick jerky movements with a flexible pointed pen dipped in ink. This form of *a* is certainly uncommon in calligraphy.

The line above should be compared with the two-line title opposite. It has a similar informality but shows the effect of holding a brush at a lower angle to produce bolder, more loosely constructed letters – a gain in vitality at the expense of legibility.

The Mars Graphic 3000 pen was used with very slight pressure to make the lines of capitals in the title shown left. The deliberate thinness of the letters expresses the message.

The soft quality of *Z* was achieved with a chinese brush, the horizontals built up from several gentle strokes.

mellow

The top and bottom examples on this page were made with the same bullet-pointed marker, evidence that writing technique can have a greater influence on the result than the instrument used. The initials are further examples of the kind of spontaneous letter made with a rounded brush (see page 43). The originals were considerably larger and it is debatable whether the righthand character, with its sprinkling of ink spots, qualifies as calligraphy at all, but nonetheless it is a recognisable letter made directly on paper with brush and ink, a graphic mark with a particular aesthetic quality.

CREATIVE
RANDOM
SPONTANEOUS
FREEFORM

Diploma

Variety within convention

The examples on this page show that even within a convention (here a flourished copperplate to head a diploma) there is room to manoeuvre. Four varieties of broad-edged pen scripts, three without flourishes, are as suitable and perhaps more contemporary in feeling than the copperplate cliché above. Blackletter, of course, is still a usual form in some European countries, not confined to antique shops, Christmas cards and legal documents. An attractive alternative to printing is the embossed letter. Dampened paper pressed over a card pattern will produce raised letters, but for more than a few copies commercial die-stamping will be necessary.

Diploma
Diploma
Diploma
Diploma

Calligraphy and type

For calligraphic forms to work in a typographic setting it is essential to use contrast, either in size, style or rendering. Most conventional typefaces – oldface, modern (types with a vertical stress and fine serifs) and sanserif – will go with calligraphic letters providing that there is a contrast in size. But it would be a mistake to use an italic script, say, with a copperplate style type (see page 38) even with a size difference, because cursive scripts from different periods do not mix well. A freely written script form, perhaps with a textured appearance, will sit happily in a typographic environment much as a drawn illustration does, and the use of large, specially designed calligraphic initial letters has a long history and is still valid today, as shown below. The capitals here are the crisply engraved face from the early nineteenth century called Walbaum.

As LONG AS WE WORK WITH THE
ARBITRARY SIGNS OF THE ALPHABET,
WE SHALL BE DEPENDENT ON THE PAST

In the expressive design shown right a large calligraphic initial is also used with type, Hermann Zapf's Optima, an instance where the familiarity of the phrase overcomes the danger of illegibility that is often present when an initial letter is treated differently from the rest of the text.

Contrast is again at work in the design above, the horizontals of the lines of type capitals (lowercase would not work so well) are a foil to the dominant script letters. The graphic impact of this design is increased by allowing the flourishes to leave the rectangle and return.

Calligraphic letters may be combined with illustrations more agreeably than would type, as below where the two short names are staggered to provide a strong interlocking pattern above the portrait of Janet Baker in a poster design. The bold horizontal rule acts both as a separating device and as a

contrast to the strong verticals of the portrait and the condensed title lettering.

Finally, calligraphy as a major feature in a page layout shows again the value of contrast, with freely written letters that dance over the narrow columns of type.

BReBR
Paaw45

Billie's Blues

SlapDash

ORIGINAL

EXTRA

Experimental scripts

The potential of brush and pen

In the combination of instrument, surface texture, hand and eye (also mind and heart) in writing letters the possibilities are endless, including the re-working of old forms and experiments in angle, slope and pressure to discover new ones. It is in this tension between eye and hand, as observed by the American teacher, Lloyd Reynolds, that fresh forms of writing develop, and we must remember that the eye may also be entranced by the hand's discoveries, leaving the mind to make a plea for legibility. A few directions are offered here in which the writer's respect for clarity has acted as a brake on wilder graphic invention, because he realises that in the graphic arts clarity of form is the normal priority.

On the opposite page the characters in the panel were made with various brushes, but the words below came from the same No. 2 brush, using different movements as indicated in the sketches. The reader will be aware by now of the role of pressure variations in such writing. In the last three designs the usual sequence of thick and thin strokes is not observed. The ascenders of *d* and *h* in *Slapdash* are kept thin to increase the liveliness of the pattern, and likewise in *Original* the usual stroke weight placing in *A* is reversed and the bowl and tail of *R* kept thin in *Extra*. There are no rules about this: the designer must decide what will work best in each case.

On this page of broad-edged pen writing the letters in the panel show several pen angles, weights and styles, while other possibilities are explored in the examples below. *Anger* was built up from several sharply made strokes of a narrow pen, the round elements becoming angular in the process. In the double stroke word below the pen's broad edge was turned onto its corners at intervals, resulting in irregular variations in the line and a slight loss of directional control. The white space enclosed by the pen strokes is very lively indeed. A very steep pen angle was used in *coteries*, a design with a strong horizontal emphasis. Usually in calligraphy the pen is pulled not pushed – the likelihood of it digging into the paper could cause ink to spatter – but with fibre-tipped pens or, as in this final example made with a balsa wood pen (see page 42), the unaccustomed pushing movements have provided changes in letterform and considerable expressive power.

Calligraphy into lettering

In this carefully pen-drawn version of an italic-based letter calligraphy has become lettering because the immediacy of pen-written letters has been replaced by the rendering of pre-planned forms, albeit calligraphic in spirit. As the diagram (right) shows, the broad-edged pen was turned from near horizontal to almost vertical to make this letterform, which mixes flat serifs with steeply arched thin strokes that mostly do not connect with the main strokes, achieving a degree of tension between the horizontal and diagonal movements. The two-stroke technique (see pages 33 and 34) allowed the waisting of each straight letter stroke to be achieved easily, and the use of ink with a resiliant steel nib rather than the fibre-tipped pens that have featured in this book helped control the finer lines.

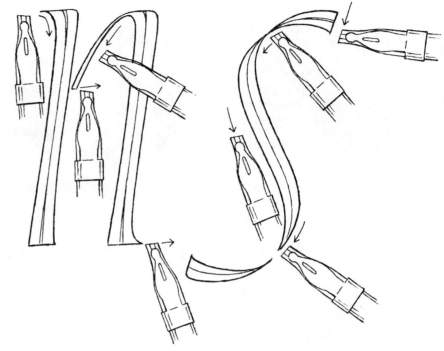

abcde

klm

Preliminary drawing established the form of each letter in this alphabet with the pen following roughly sketched outlines. It is important to stress that the drawing was done with full understanding of what the pen could do, so that the design which was carefully planned by drawing was cal-ligraphically conceived, with drawing and writing interacting creatively. To achieve an informal effect the letters were drawn/written without horizontal guidelines, and the usual lower serif of ƒ left off to improve the letter pattern in this arrangement.

The italic alphabet lacks matching capital letters, but in this display they are set between contrasting torn paper capitals whose origins lie in typographic forms. A stencil effect (essential in the torn paper letters) unifies these very contrasting styles in which smooth contrasts with rough and bold contrasts with light. Three strands of contemporary lettering – the written, the drawn and the typographic – are brought together here symbolising their interdependence.

ABCD
efghij
KLMN
opqrst
UVWX
yǵz
&

2

Drawing
and
design

The drawing hand

The calligrapher is used to manipulating a broad pen to make letters with disciplined fingers controlling the formation of characters whose shapes derive from centuries of development. In this development the natural movements of the writing hand were a major influence on letter design sometimes allowing great freedom in dexterous and lively scripts, sometimes, as in some forms of black-letter, being severely controlled to produce angular formal writing.

The inscriptional roman capital was first painted on the stone in a sequence of skilful brush strokes, giving the geometrically proportioned forms the elegance and subtlety that arises naturally from sophisticated brush manipulation. Unfortunately the dead hand of geometrical drawing has usually made the drawn roman capital a stiff parody of its originally living forms. Renaissance writing manuals abound with complex and awkward diagrams of roman capitals, and the practice of using ruled straight lines and compass arcs still survives today.

The hand can be made to draw dead-straight lines, with or without the use of a ruler, but this is to deny it the chance to apply a natural grace to the drawing. If the fingers are allowed their full range of movement a pencil drawing vertical and horizontal strokes produces lines with a degree of curve, as the illustrations on this page show. This curvature can be very slight, not even leading into serifs, and the lines can be made in a series of short strokes rather than in one sweep. Drawing in this way is best done with the hand remaining in one position while the fingers control the pencil's travel. The following pages show this technique applied to diagonals and to curves.

This demonstration of freehand drawing is necessarily very simple and only seeks to show the principle of allowing the fingers to control the drawing of basic letter strokes. In practice every kind of manipulation is used to produce letters that accord with the designer's intention and mental image and the typical letter-forms that illustrate this technique were drawn with a variety of fibre-tipped and metal-nibbed pens. What is certain is that drawing letters in this way will lead to the development of a *drawn* style that is different from a *calligraphic* style and eventually the possible emergence of a distinctive personal style that is rooted in the individual hand's particular skill. As a personal handwriting style can emerge even when following strict models, so too can a personal lettering style.

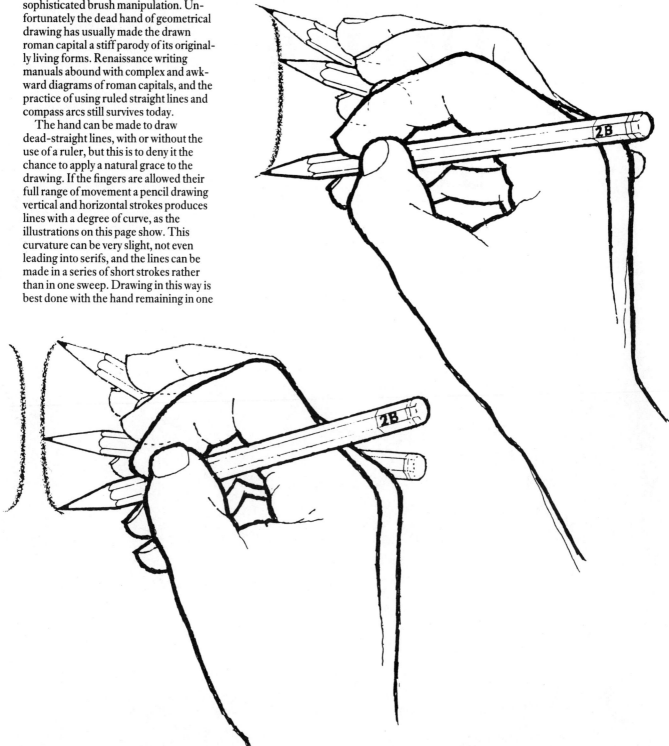

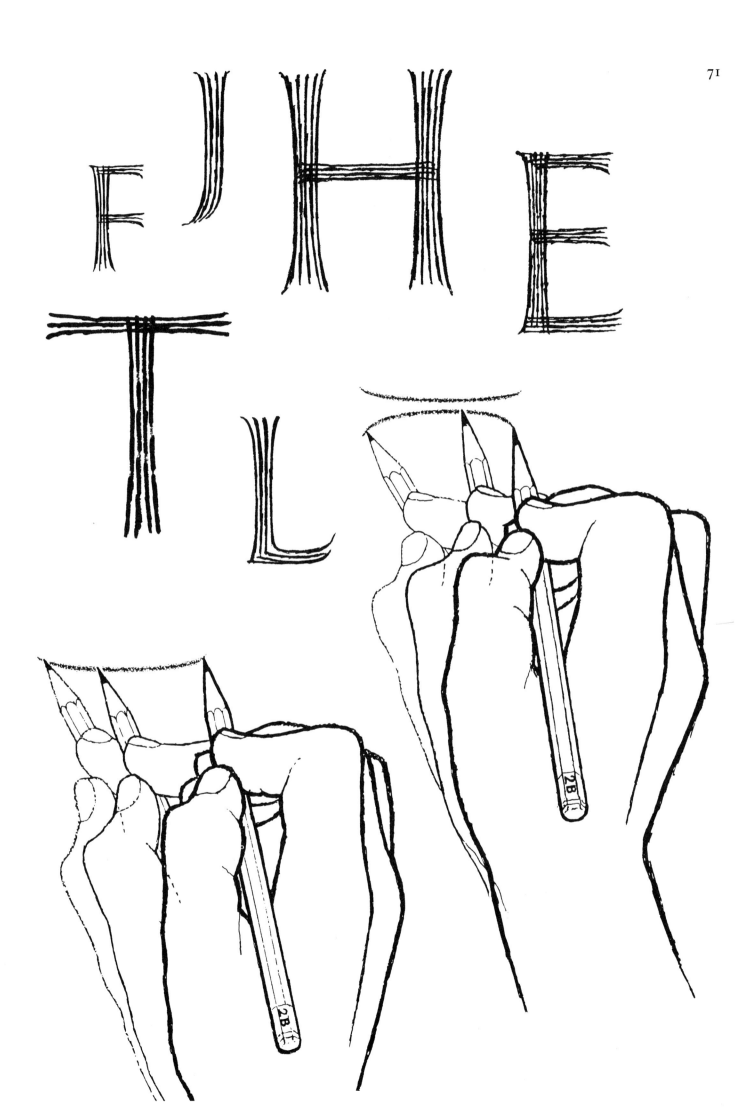

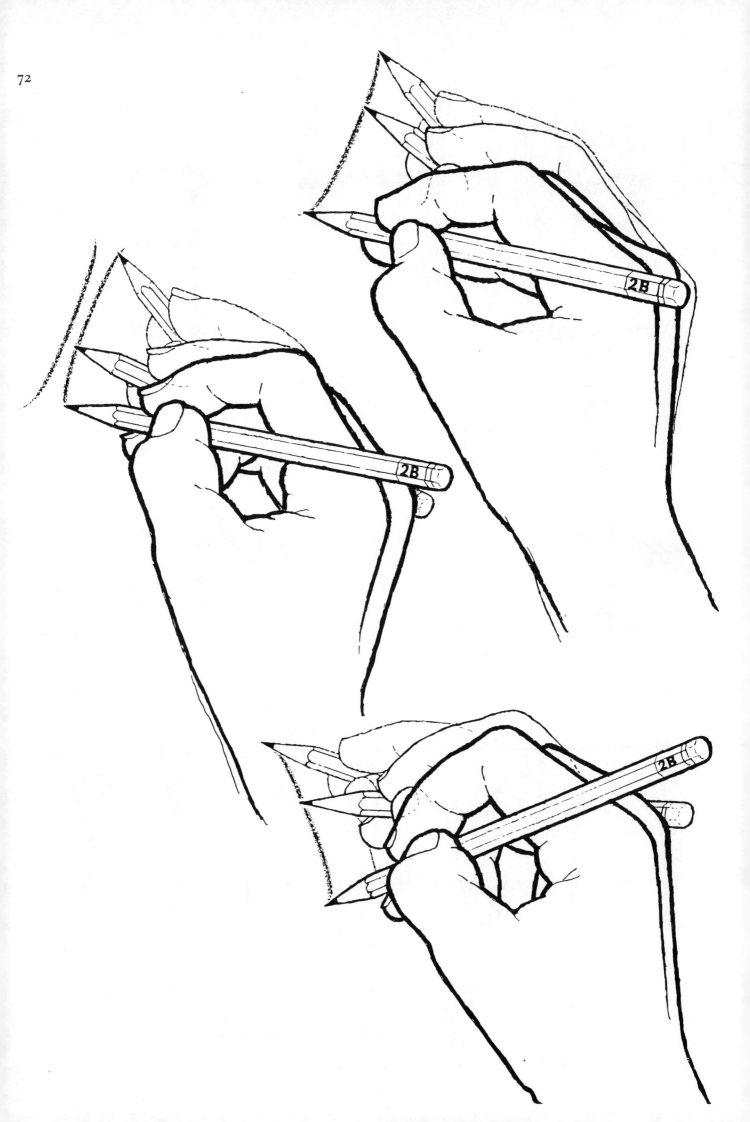

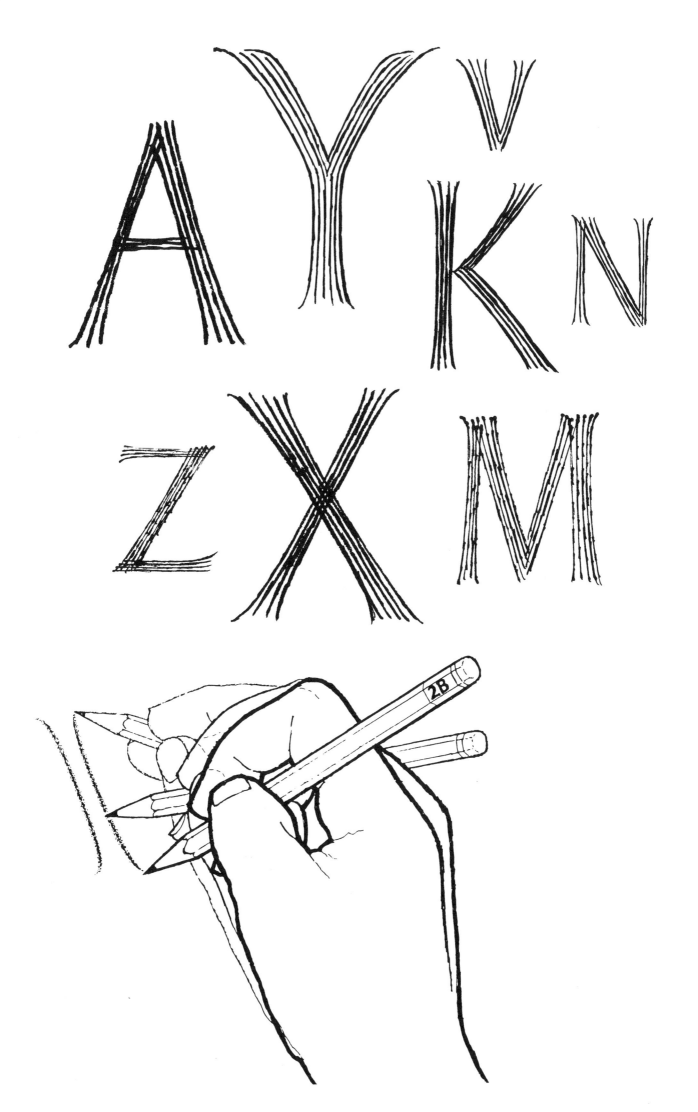

74

The alphabet of capital letters on pages 76 and 77 shows the build up of each character from a sequence of lines. Serifs grow gracefully from the strokes and do not appear to have been applied separately as often happens when drawing instruments have been used. The sketchy drawing is based on well proportioned letters and the conventional disposition of thick and thin strokes has been followed. The size of letter is within the scope of the fingers' range of movement, with the hand moving progressively from left to right as the letters build up.

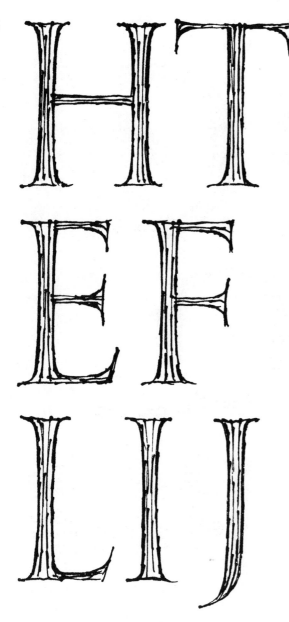

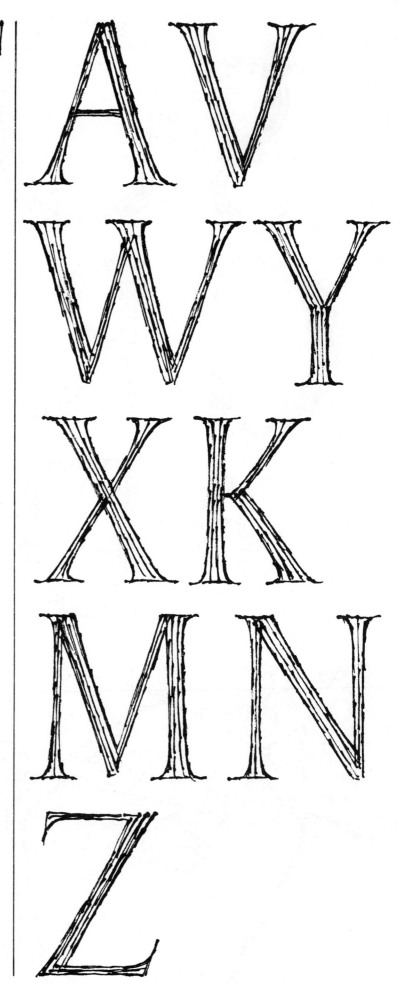

Capital letters

Letters E, F and L are narrow. Notice the curve on the inside of the bottom junction in E and L, also the angled serif terminating the lower horizontals, both of which derive from brush writing, (see Catich: *The Origin of the Serif*). The central horizontals of E and F are fractionally shorter than the upper ones, while the lower horizontal of E is longer. J descends below the base line.

Diagonals dominate the group of letters on the right. A has a flat top. The Vs that make up W are narrowed to avoid the letter becoming too wide. X and K are narrow, narrower at the top than the bottom, and the verticals of M are splayed to avoid cramping the inner spaces. Both M and N are strengthened with serifs on the top apexes, unlike some classical examples, and the bottom horizontal of Z has an angled serif that matches E and L.

Letters O and Q are narrower than true circles and the full height curves have the stress of calligraphic strokes. D has an inside curve on the bottom junction that matches E and L. Above are the narrow letters that use half-height curved strokes. The bowl of P is open and the simple form of R lacks the connecting stroke. B has the inside curve on the bottom junction that matches E, L and D, and like S is narrower at the top. S is made from the blending of left and right curves.

IMPERIAL
PRINT

First-century capitals show the influence of brush writing in the variations of stroke width and serif formation. M has pointed apexes, a detail rarely seen in printing types.

Many sixteenth-century reconstructions of the roman capital were made, using geometry both as an analytical basis and an aid to drawing. The results were often crude and complicated, as this sketch shows, but researches into the long-neglected roman capital influenced the contemporary development of the first roman printing types.

The sixteenth-century type of Nicolas Jenson preserved the roman capital for the printed page, a translation from carved stone to cast metal that required a strengthening of the form, particularly the serifs. Roman capitals continue to survive in the form of printing type.

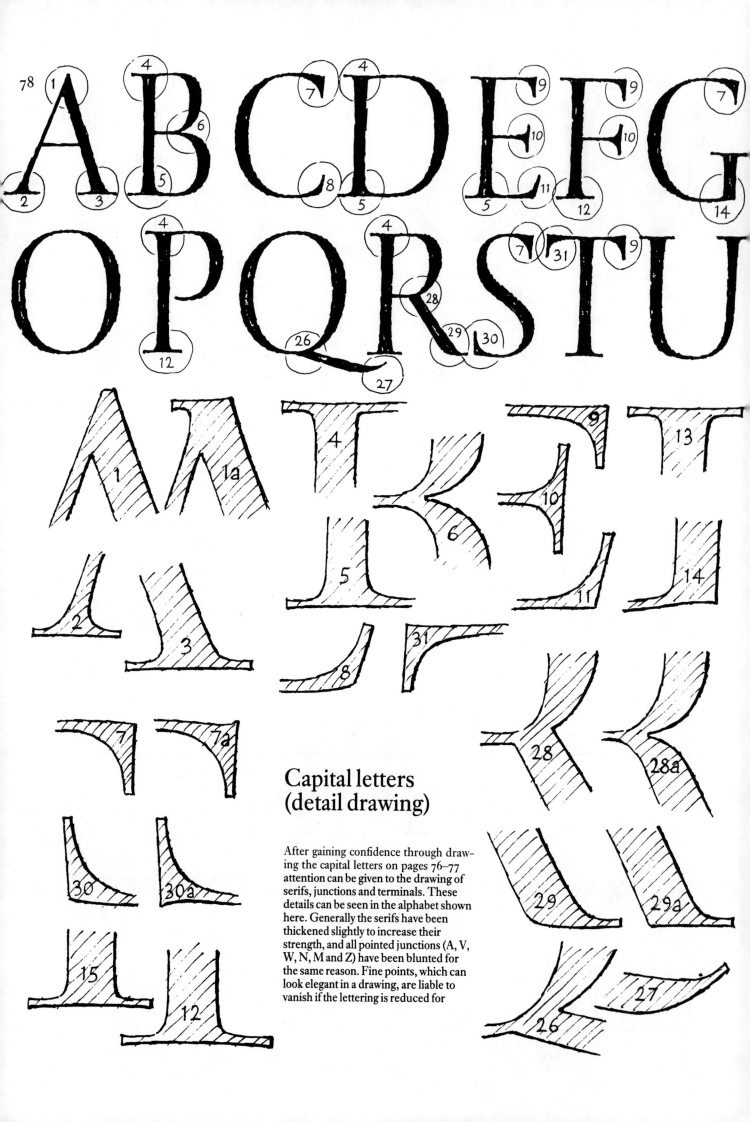

Capital letters
(detail drawing)

After gaining confidence through drawing the capital letters on pages 76–77 attention can be given to the drawing of serifs, junctions and terminals. These details can be seen in the alphabet shown here. Generally the serifs have been thickened slightly to increase their strength, and all pointed junctions (A, V, W, N, M and Z) have been blunted for the same reason. Fine points, which can look elegant in a drawing, are liable to vanish if the lettering is reduced for

reproduction. Allow for this and strengthen the drawing accordingly. The marked contrast between thick and thin strokes will help the designer to grasp the form of the characters more easily than from letters with slight contrast.

Details are shown in enlarged drawings, sometimes with alternative treatments. Typical horizontal terminals to thick and thin vertical strokes (13, 15, 23, 24) occur frequently and are not circled in the alphabet above. A study of these enlargements will assist in appreciation and drawing of the roman capital alphabet, laying the foundations for mastering other styles of lettering. For more detailed information see Type design, pages 114–119.

Letterform variations (capital letters)

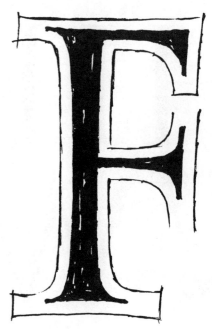

The drawn outline gives almost unlimited possibilities for the creation of letterform variations, a minute number of which are shown on the following pages. Degree of curvature of 'straight' strokes, contrast between thick and thin strokes, letter weight, i.e., boldness or lightness, serif design, are all at the lettering designer's command. So far in this book only conventional roman capital forms have been described, but here we can look at some developments of those forms, typographic as well as calligraphic, which can be re-made by the drawing hand.

The first line of letters below shows a more typographic version of the basic roman capital, with strong extended serifs. The letters in the next line are bolder but the serifs are much finer than in the first example. Letters which derive from eighteenth-century type, whose very prominent serifs swell from the hairline thin strokes, are shown in the third line. Freehand drawing gives the usually dead-straight verticals extra life and elegance. The last line shows a re-drawing of the nineteenth-century Egyptian letterform; strong and massive but when drawn in outline surprisingly delicate.

FGNSAQ

SAEMP

MEDRV

TEDJK

ANWESRTU

Without guidelines and free from the constraint of horizontal serifs the line of lettering above has some of the vitality and freshness of swift drawing. A E M, slightly condensed with some weight contrast, have splayed stroke endings which are not quite serifs. The typeface Optima is somewhat in this style. S N P are bolder and wider letters in which the junctions of N have been widened to create extra inner space, and the bowl of P deepened to reduce the space below. The bottom line of letters has, like the other examples, shaped vertical and horizontal strokes of almost identical weight. The stroke endings are slightly angled to give the characters a discreet forward motion.

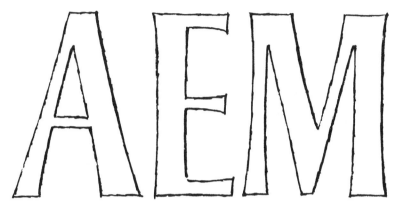

AEM

SNP

FATCRSN

82

The liveliness of calligraphic forms provides the basis for lettering described here, with the drawn line following and extending the pen's characteristic marks. When most other horizontal serifs are suppressed the lead-in serif at the top left of many written letters and the final right-hand serif give a directional movement that is largely absent in roman capitals. This left to right flow given by the 'east-bound serif', as Paul Standard

has aptly named it, can be emphasised by other subtle drawn devices. Vertical strokes and diagonals may have bottom left and top right endings square-cut or slightly rounded, and diagonals may be given very slight curves to add extra movement. Vertical serifs can vary considerably in treatment, ranging from normal serifs gently swept back to the upswept endings characteristic of the lifted pen. The result of this editing and

development is a calligraphically inspired line of great flexibility and potential; the letter's edge is manipulated to suit the designer's vision and his control of the drawn letter is absolute, as shown in these outline capitals.

In the line above the flow between letters is increased by extending under or over their neighbours, and by the use of the lowercase form of Y. Curved strokes can be strengthened and given extra visual energy if drawn with a pronounced stress, as shown in D, with the horizontal beginning of the stroke drawn out before its descent. Tension and liveliness are increased when letters are condensed giving the enclosed spaces a feeling of compressed energy.

Creative control of the edge of letters reaches its most adventurous and free-ranging potential in the fluid line of *art nouveau* letterforms. These styles, often far removed from broad-edged pen letters, offer to the experienced designer a rich source of graphic ideas which can be adapted and incorporated into his drawing. Sinuous line and movement characterise these letterforms and the resulting flexibility can be used to create decorative and well-integrated groups of letters. Serifs may become positive, decorative elements, growing to fill the spaces within a letter or word, or vivaciously extending letters into the surrounding space, as the calligrapher's swash letters do.

Roundness and flow − these attributes will change quite plain, static letters into lively forms. Serifs and corners may be rounded to make letters usually angular appear soft, and in bold condensed letters the spaces between take on a positive life of their own when seen against the letter's mass.

Lowercase roman and italic letters

The drawing of minuscule characters, whose broad-edged pen basis is shown far left, should be preceded by practising the left to right strokes illustrated here.

Although maintaining a calligraphic flavour the design relationship of these letters to the roman capitals on pages 76–77 is obvious in the treatment of the double horizontal serifs.

The Carolingian minuscule of the ninth century was part of the slow process by which writing styles evolved from roman capitals. Its temporary eclipse by blackletter in most parts of Europe was ended by its revival by scholars and printers of the Renaissance. The printer's term for type that is derived from the minuscule letter is lowercase. Our understanding today of the calligraphic form underlying type is largely due to Edward Johnston's research, writing and teaching.

minuscule
lowercase

The pen angle, the gentle slope and the letters' compressed forms give italic its distinctive flattened curves, steeply up-swept junctions and serifs, and rhythmic grace. The basic elements converted to drawn lines are shown here and may be followed for drawing practice.

Calligraphy

The fifteenth-century script used in the Papal chanceries, known today as italic, was adopted by printers and thus became with roman capitals and lower-case the third element in the main typographic tradition of the Western world. Its revival in this century as a

handwriting style has given new life to this elegant script, and facsimiles of manuals by Renaissance writing masters like Arrighi – his woodcut version of italic is shown here – continue to inspire contemporary designers.

Lowercase roman and italic letters (detail drawing)

Lowercase and italic letters are shown here in more finished form, and details and some alternatives are given in the enlarged drawings. It is essential to understand the calligraphic nature of these letters and useful, if in doubt, to practise writing them with a broad-edged pen. Many horizontal and vertical serifs are similar to those detailed for capital letters on pages 78–79, while detail 3 shows the single, angled, top serif to some vertical stems.

Although calligraphy is the basis of these two separate alphabets much of the detail is typographic in origin, such as the alternative ball endings to a, r, j and y.

The drawing hand also adds its own subtleties in softened corners, carefully controlled serifs and such details as the scooped out triangle at the top of t which reduces the blackness of the pen form.

In italic, the most cursive of the letterforms described in this book, it is especially important to retain a calligraphic movement — the slight thickening of junctions characteristic of the angled pen's upsweep, steep serif angle, compressed form and the twisted ribbon effect made by the strokes as they swell and thin. The general point made about strengthening serifs on roman capitals also applies to the lowercase and italic alphabets.

Letterform variations (lowercase letters)

The stress that derives from the pen angle should generally be respected in all variations on letters, as in the shallow tilt to top left serifs and in the arch springing from vertical stems in several letters, with maximum thickness at the top right of the curve. Calligraphic stress can be maintained to give vitality to virtually even weight and almost sans-serif letters, or emphasised as in this condensed lowercase version of the east-bound serif letter. A fluid line and increased contrast between thick and thin strokes provides further variations in lowercase forms.

enabfpy
nabustejd

The forms of italic script can be emphasised or transformed by drawing, either given a rounder appearance or a highly compressed angularity that rivals blackletter. In the sequence below the inside shape of *a* maintains its distinctive identity as the letters are compressed, drawn very bold and finally sketched in a series of vigorous, quickly rendered nearly straight lines. As with other letters described on previous pages the drawn line controls the character to create the desired effect, whether it be flowing elegance, elegant strength or rugged vitality.

abcdefg

abcde

abcde

abcde

Aspects of the drawn letter

The alphabets on pages 76–77 and 84–85 were built up from a sequence of lines giving some indication of the characters' substance, but drawing letters in outline – the usual preliminary to inking them in – requires an understanding of the relationship between line and form. The sequence shown below illustrates this relationship. The B is drawn from left to right: first the left-hand edge is drawn; then the stem thickness assessed by eye and the inside shapes of the bowls drawn in; the outline is then completed and the space contained within the outline reads as B. Moving on, the space between B and the next character is assessed, the first line of this letter is drawn and the stages repeated until BA is complete. In practice more lines may be sketched in but this illustration indicates the visual judgement that is necessary when drawing letters in outline, and the truth of the statement that 'a line has two sides' – while you are drawing one form (the letter) you are also defining another (the space around or inside the letter).

If a line has two sides it also has thickness and this thickness, however slight, must be allowed for if the outline letter is to be filled in. The illustrations here show how unexpectedly bold the filled-in letters look compared with their outline, and how much thinner they look when the background is filled in, absorbing the letters' outlines. The designer, usually working on positive letters, must be sure to keep the outlines of letters *within* the desired stroke width.

Drawing letters from the inside

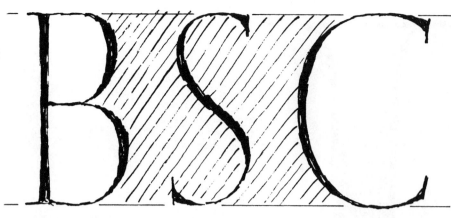

An alternative to drawing outline letters, with their lack of substance, is to sketch the skeleton first, like an armature, and to build up the weight until the final outline or edge is determined. This technique makes the assessment of inter-letter space easier, and if the sketchiness is maintained a pleasing rough edge can be achieved with flecks of white showing through the letter that is reminiscent of a printed type image photographically enlarged. Try this technique using fibre-tipped pens or brush and ink, keeping any preliminary pencil sketching to a mini-mum (or dispense with pencil altogether). Use short scribbled strokes to build up the letters. A worn-down brush or fibre-tipped pen that no longer makes precise marks is ideal for this kind of drawing. It prevents over-tight work.

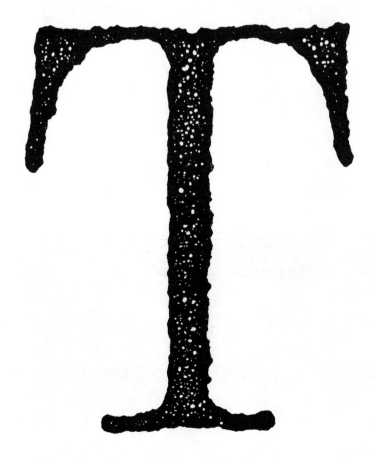

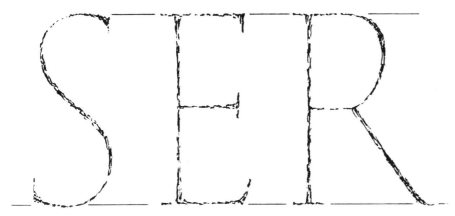

Drawing the background around the letter

Although negative lettering is usually drawn positive and photographically reversed this is an illuminating exercise because it increases the perception of letter shapes. Begin by lightly sketching the barest skeletons in pencil, then paint the background gradually enclosing the letter. When the letter stands out clearly the pencil lines can be erased. Letters drawn in this way tend to be bolder and the serifs stronger than positively drawn letters.

The awareness of the inner spaces of letters derived from the exercise described above can be exploited to make strong graphic designs of letterforms.

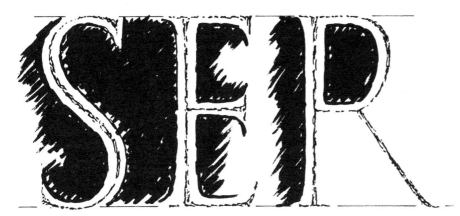

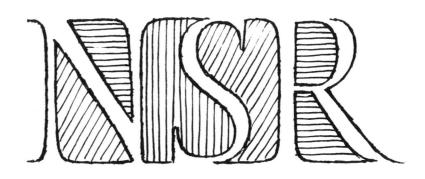

The reader, familiar with letters drawn in outline from the many illustrations in this book, may perhaps be attracted by their appearance of lightness and elegance. Note too, that the outline is often not of a uniform thickness. A lively variation of weight gives an illusion of depth. This effect suggests a third dimension. The first version of the word

Outline is drawn in a fine, even line, while below can be seen a similar drawing with extra thickness added consistently to the right and underside edges, suggesting a third dimension and adding to the lettering's vitality. Consistency is important here; imagine the sun at a particular position and the shadows it would cast. In the word

Thistle the thin parts of the letters are drawn in single lines, giving a lighter, more calligraphic effect.

The implied shadow can be made to dominate, as here in these initials, which are shown photographically reduced to mark the degree to which line weight diminishes in reduction.

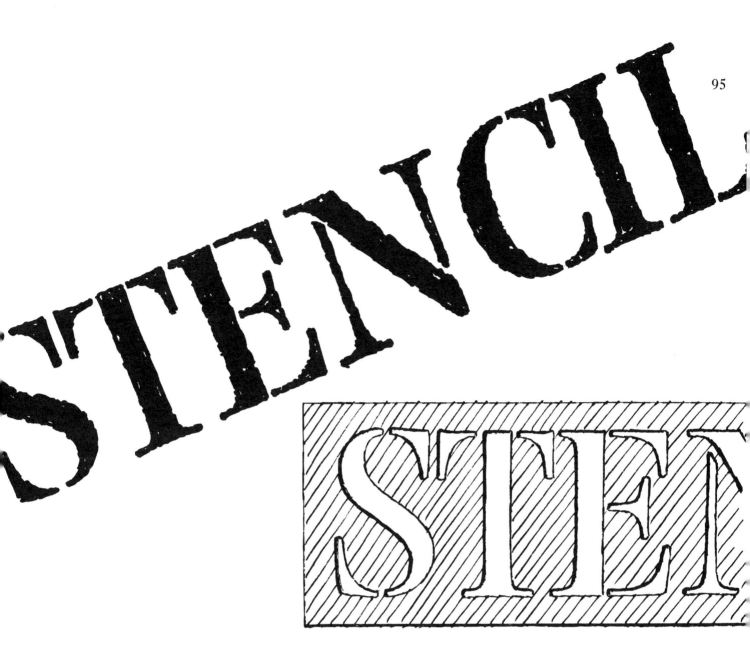

Stencil letters

Stencil lettering, in which the characters are broken at intervals, has a graphic attraction that can be exploited for its own sake. Disconnecting the elements of stroke, curve and serif that make up individual letters adds a sparkle to even the most formal characters.

The stencil effect lends itself readily to calligraphic forms, where the separate pen strokes provide natural breaks.

Drawing
for reproduction

Lettering designed for reproduction is normally drawn in black waterproof ink on white line board (or line paper, which can be used on a lightbox to trace off a preliminary design and can be cut up to correct any spacing faults), and may be drawn full size or in a larger size for reduction. Drawing at the finished size has the great advantage that every detail of weight and serif can be easily assessed. Drawing at a larger size is useful if the reproduced size is to be very small. Photographic reduction will minimise any roughness in the drawing. However, it is more difficult to judge the weight of the finished letters because their mass will reduce at twice the rate of their linear measurement – a letter reduced to half its height will occupy only one quarter of its original area – and unless this is allowed for by increasing the weight of the drawn letter the final result may well look disappointingly thin. An accurate solution to this problem is to make preliminary drawings at the finished size and to enlarge these on an enlarging projector, tracing the projected image carefully onto line paper.

The drawing of finished artwork can be divided into four stages.

1. With the aid of horizontal guidelines the letters are sketched freehand in outline using a medium soft pencil. During this stage and the next the work should be kept horizontal, so that the shapes of the letters and the spaces between can be accurately assessed.

2. Using a pointed brush (No. 2 or 3), the drawn outlines are filled in with black waterproof ink, but the ink is not taken right up to the edges of the letters. Final edge definition and weight control is left to the next stage.

3. A technical pen, here an 0.2 Rotring, is used to smooth the edges, filling in the irregularities left from the brush-inking. It is now an advantage to move the work around to help drawing control. Particular attention is given to the definition of serifs and the junction in r. Final, minute adjustments can now be made to the letters, then all pencil work erased but the guidelines re-drawn ready for the last stage.

4. Using white gouache and a fine brush the shakes that inevitably occur in freehand drawing are removed, giving the letters their final polish before being photographed for reproduction. All guidelines should now be erased.

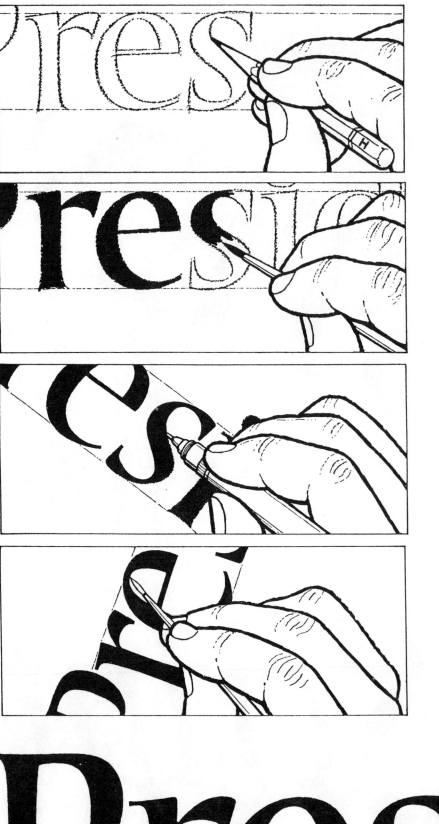

If the preliminary pencil drawing is kept sketchy the inked letters can be shaped directly by the brush, spacing adjusted accordingly and alternative forms substituted to improve the letter pattern. Final drawing can then follow the procedure described in stages 3 and 4 opposite.

Lettering drawn on paper can be cut up and the words accurately re-assembled in any desirable arrangement. Spacing faults can be remedied too, and unsatisfactory characters re-drawn and substituted.

In the design of lettering the important factors of meaning, pattern, legibility, material and technique make demands, and a balance has to be found. Here we can only concern ourselves with a few examples of the formal aspects of lettering.

The condensed capitals (right) form a rectangle in which the potentially disruptive LA combination has been brought under control by narrowing the L and adding a top serif to the A. Space between other letters has been kept open, the unusual form of Y allows extra inner space and the S extends back into the space behind.

Below, expanded capitals, helped by thin rules and decorative space-filling points, flank a line of larger, bold, condensed capitals. In condensed lettering, especially roman capitals, the usual differences in letter width are largely eliminated and wide letters such as O and D are considerably compressed, while letters with diagonals such as M and N need to have their junctions widened to maintain inner space.

VERSE
PLAYS

HENRY·WOOD
PROMENADE
◄CONCERTS►

Traders' Diary

The initials above have been reduced so that the lowercase letters can be as large as possible and inter-line space can be kept to a minimum. In the ra combination the bowl of a extends slightly into the space under r, and where r meets y the fit between the letters is improved by curving r under the serif of y and bringing the tail around to enclose the space — joining the letters would look contrived.

Creative Lettering

An italic version of this book's title shows that when joining *ti* and *tt* the horizontal connections should not be allowed to dominate — as can happen in broad-edged pen calligraphy — and a space-saving relationship of *ri*. Both capitals are lowered, allowing the upsweep of *C* to lead into the word and let the *L* slip under.

100

The arrangement of a quotation from William Morris on this page uses a condensed upright letterform stacked in tightly packed lines, ranging from the left. Careful spacing of the third and fourth lines avoids the equal length that would be out of place in this arrangement of unequal lines. The italic form of *a* is used because its simple compressed shape works best in this situation. In the sixth line y is drawn with its tail contained within the line of letters to avoid a clash with the ascender of k below, while k is the italic form to reduce the space on its right. To maintain the vertical emphasis of these letters t uses an extension of its vertical instead of the usual triangle.

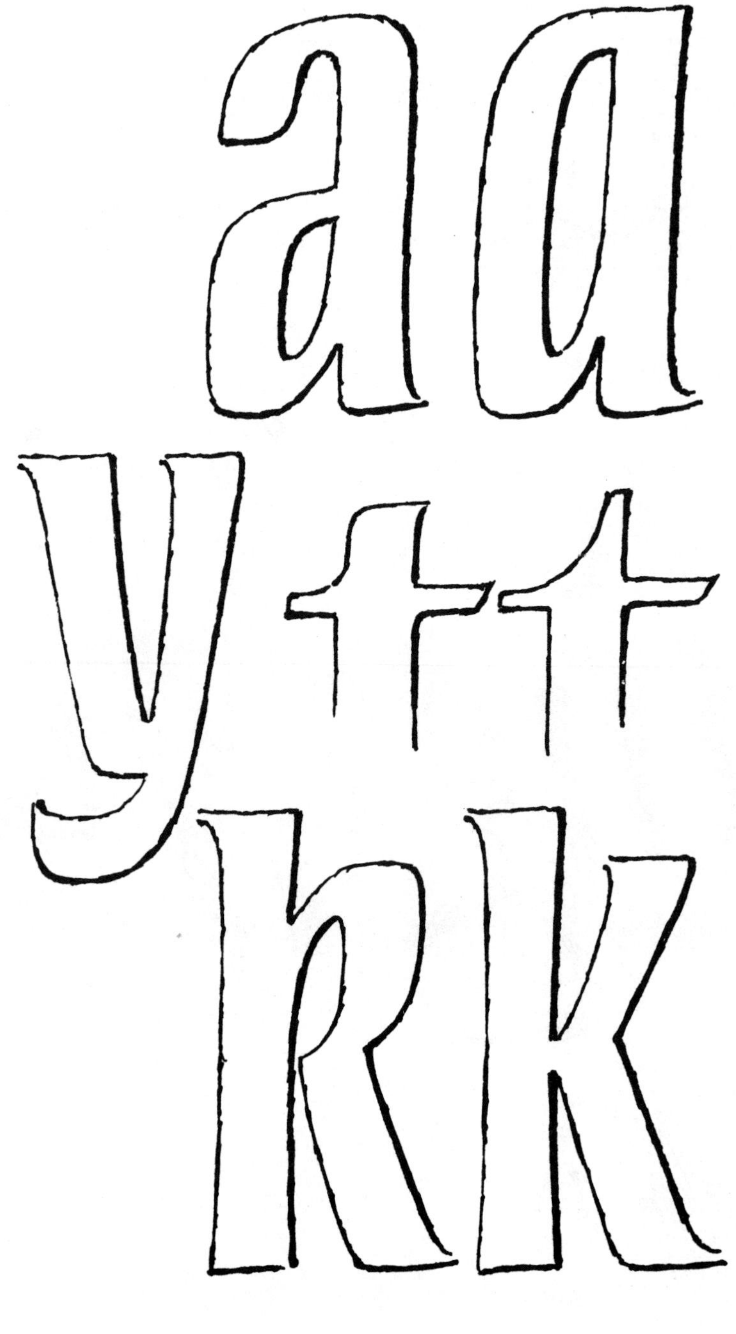

a a

y t t

r k

Have nothing in your houses that you do not know to be useful or believe to be beautiful

BRANKSOME GALLERY
DANIEL CHARTERIS
SCULPTURE & PAINTING 1972-79

Here is a rectangle of freely-drawn capitals, using different sizes of letter to achieve a common line length. To add curves to what would otherwise be a pattern dominated by straight lines the unusual round E is used, and crossbars are added to the tops of As to strengthen the horizontal line. In the top line G and Y are a little unusual. The lowercase form of Y helps to reduce the space after R and the horizontal bar on G provides a visual link with the central arm of E.

Below is an asymmetric arrangement of three words, carefully placed so that ascenders and descenders do not clash. The flourishes add liveliness and balance to the design.

Apple blossom time

Lettering drawn on a curve is an attractive solution to some design problems, especially where space is narrow, and here two words are usefully linked in a curved design. Some distortion is inevitable to achieve a convincing effect, and for this reason it is rarely possible simply to arrange straight letters on a curve. The letters in the top word have been widened slightly at the top and narrowed slightly at the bottom; A has a bridging serif and is allowed to join R at the bottom, while the bowl of R is spread to the right. In the bottom word where the curve runs the other way the reverse happens; the letters are widened at the bottom and usually wide letters like T are narrowed to achieve a good fit with their neighbours.

CRISIS
POINT

The lively pattern of letters shown
above is achieved by controlling the
balance between the letters and the inner
spaces. Precision is needed in the drawing and letters are allowed to touch or
nearly touch according to the designer's
judgement. The bottom line of spaced
out capitals is a good foil to the vigorous
pattern above.

Upright letters marching uphill require a distortion of their curved strokes
that brings the main thickness higher on
the right and lower on the left. Here
extended strokes help to complete the
pattern.

Monogram design

The combination of two or more initials into a single, compact design requires an appreciation of letterforms as graphic symbols and the ability to achieve a marriage in which the individual characters harmonise without loss of identity. It is best to look for what is on offer in the letters, relying on quite subtle manipulation of form, weight and serif, avoiding designs that appear forced or contrived. There is no need to over-embellish the design with flourishing and intertwining.

In designing a monogram for the Thimble Press, a publisher of books about writing for children, several sketches led to the idea of using lowercase, or small letters, to symbolise the company's activities. The initials t p were linked emphasising the curve of t, the scooped-out top of t provided another curve, and the descender of p was made

very short. A complementary octagonal shape made possible a reversed version of the design. The finished drawing with reduced and reversed versions are shown below.

The publisher's device BH (shown opposite), designed to appear on title pages and book spines, had to be in several styles to suit different typographic settings. The difference in width between the usually narrow B and wide H had to be lessened, especially in the two-line versions designed for narrow spines.

CREA, the initials for a centre for research into applied aesthetics, employs outline capitals, the A angled to allow room for the centre dot and a line box added to contain the design.

An intricate combination of W and two numerals, designed for pierced metal, uses overlapping to lower the cross-over

point and provide extra strength, while rounded serifs and inner corners facilitate fret-sawing.

A combination of the QE, a publisher's device, adopts a small e so that both characters can share the same shape. The short calligraphic extension to the right aids legibility.

The author's monogram MH, shown here in an early sans serif version and the later, strongly serifed designs, physically links the two letters and uses deep shadow to symbolise his inscriptional work while the open-ended serifs add an appropriate graphic touch.

The double L L, short for Lulu, is carved in slate and uses swash letters originating in copperplate scripts to fit the diamond shape.

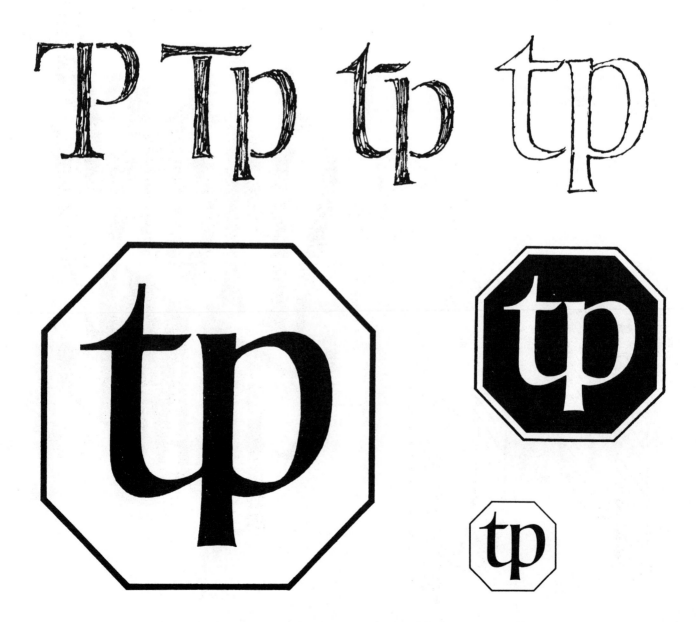

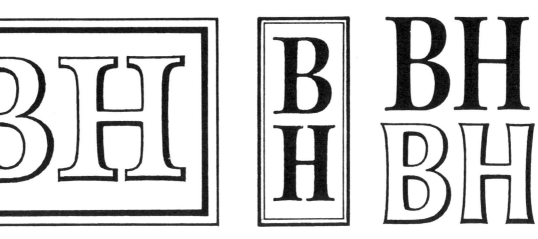

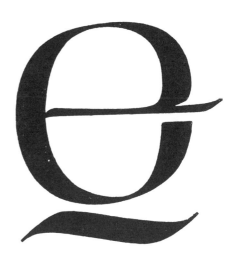

Any distinctively drawn and styled name or title is a logotype — a word or words designed to be used in perhaps a variety of ways to identify a person, activity or product. The sequence of sketches below shows the search for a style of letter to illustrate the distinctive, swirling lines of marbled paper. A fragment of typical marbled pattern is reproduced. The final design, in which outlines of varying thickness flow and merge to create a dancing script, is displayed in various sizes and arrangements.

Opposite, the lettering for the collected edition of the works of the Brazilian author Machado de Assis uses swash initials partly outlined to link the two lines of this design. A poster title for a Pre-Raphaelite exhibition is drawn with a hint of the kind of medieval calligraphy admired by those artists — in lettering that aims to evoke a period or style a hint is often all that is required. Another poster title, for Thomas Gainsborough, uses a backswept flourish to contain the first name. Young Drama, a magazine title,

uses the lowercase y to link the two lines of capitals, and another title, Signal, features a long-tailed g and a dropped initial in a line of stencil letters. Both designs also appear in lighter, outline versions for use on stationery.

Machado
de Assis

The
Pre-Raphaelites

Thomas
Gainsborough

Signal Signal

YOUNG
DRAMA

YOUNG
DRAMA

The private individual wanting an attractively lettered label to identify his books is often drawn to the appearance of italic reversed out of a solid background, a style made fashionable by such masters as Reynolds Stone. Flourishes can make a useful contribution but should not be allowed to strangle the design. Because the lettering will be small it is sensible to draw the original at a larger size, taking care to allow for the effects of reduction.

The first sketch for John Neal's bookplate used the familiar oval shape, but the idea of stacking his names and splitting Book-seller offered more interesting possibilities, including the addition of an address when the design was adapted for use on stationery. Several sketches on this theme are shown, with the finished drawing and printed label. The solid background need not be black, but in any colour that is dark enough in tone to show the negative letters effectively.

Three versions of Pat England's bookplate fit the lettering into an almost square design, using hyphenation, ligatures and triangular dots to fill the space. The traditional Latin Ex Libris is used decoratively to contrast with the names in the rectangular bookplate for Frederick Stevenson, and in a panel with concave corners the ampersand links the short names Hugh and Jane.

Including the address on Graham Greene's bookplate was an opportunity to encircle the names with capitals.

Barbara Gathercole's rather long second name is shortened as it curves around the oval's lower edge, and complementary flourishes above make a setting for Barbara's contrasting italic. In the finished drawing, shown actual size, a solid area defines the oval background that will appear positive when photographically reversed.

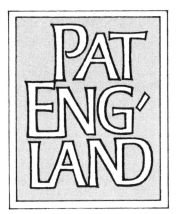

Bookjacket design

Publishing's need for attractive jackets to help market books gives the designer a unique opportunity to combine language and letters. The creative possibilities are endless, even though commissions are usually limited to three colours, an upright format and strict editorial requirements. And the spine of the jacket, with its narrow, upright rectangle, tightly filled with information, provides a further challenge.

Through thumbnail sketches which explore different arrangements of the author's name and title, a satisfactory design evolves. Sometimes the final balance of the elements needs careful adjustment, as in this design for *The Canterbury Tales* which uses a calligraphic letter for the title with plain initials. The

compressed verticals of the title are relieved by well-spaced capitals and horizontal rules.

The bookjacket's narrowness encourages condensed lettering, exemplified here in *Studies of Aeschylus* which uses a letter drawn from the roman rustic of the fifth century. The graceful vigour of the lettering is set off by the space below.

Stories up to a Point, using the same letter throughout, makes a strong pattern in which the title is defined by a partial outline and a second colour. The slope to the right is balanced by S and swash extensions to B and the second P (a swash on the first P would be too much of a good thing).

The brutality of a prison revolt is suggested in *A Time to Die* by tough letters

that break through the edges of the design. Stark black and white emphasise this drama.

Pre-classical capitals arranged asymmetrically give an appropriate flavour to *The Study of Greek Inscriptions*, helped by the breaking of the final word in the title.

The surprise of lines tilting and running off the edges gives *A Tale of Love, Alas* its impact. Here title and author are usefully separated by a line of smaller, white capitals.

Great simplicity, the use of a single word for the main feature and plenty of space give *Saki* an advantage over books with longer titles. On the wide spine the title runs across and is joined by the publisher's device, a feature usually placed at the foot of the spine.

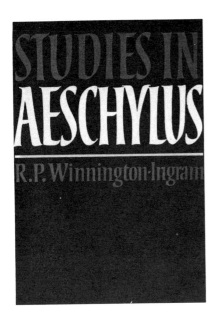

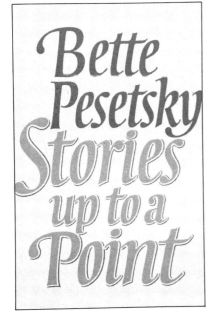

III

The designer should grasp every opportunity and in *The Voice of Experience* the space within the title neatly accepts the book's sub-title, which is emphasised with bold rules. The resulting rectangle of lettering is visually centred on the jacket.

Considerable variation in letter proportion was required to achieve the deceptive simplicity of *Ulysses*; the title being comparatively condensed and all the lettering the same height.

Short words can be a problem, but in *The Shakespeare Play as Poem* they are arranged to give prominence to the important longer word. The strong vertical stress of this upright script letter is complemented by the single line of capitals.

Several idiosyncratic touches give a very slight Hebraic flavour to *The Exagoge of Ezekiel*, and the descending tails of *Exagoge* are drawn down providing a link with the second half of the title.

Overspel, a novel about adultery, uses the uncial E in the title, and a shadow to suggest double life. The author stands back from this complexity and the word *Roman* (novel) provides a useful balancing element.

In lettering that fills the jacket, as in *The Honorary Consul*, some letters will inevitably join their neighbours. In this design Greene is emphasised by larger lettering and the panel with a white border reinforces the design.

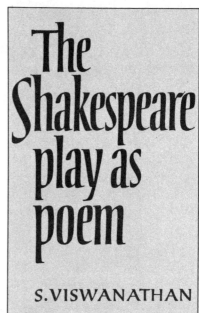

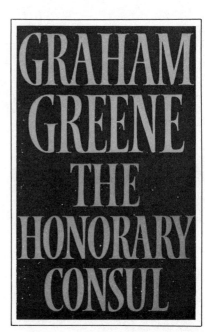

The usually narrow area of the spine of the jacket can require some ingenuity to achieve a good fit to the lettering. Most spine lettering must be specially drawn; it is rarely satisfactory simply to reduce it from the front of the jacket. Amongst the spines shown here that for *Magical Thought in Creative Writing* has very short capitals and descenders within a narrow space, and the author's name fitted in alongside the second descender. *Aristotle & Logical Theory* uses the space-saving ampersand, and in both *Op de rug van vuile zwanen* and *Worldly Goods* the author's names occupy two lines to allow more space for the title lettering. *Een vlucht regenwulpen* has space for generous ascenders and descenders, with the capitals of the author's name being the same height as the title's lowercase. The title and author appear in two closely spaced groups on the spine of *The Good Son*, the short words allowing a horizontal setting.

The creation of a typeface family in which individual characters work together in groups while retaining their individuality, is perhaps the greatest challenge to the skill of the lettering designer. Type design has technical aspects that cannot be dealt with here, so what follows is a description of the conceptual and drawing stages of a roman alphabet, capitals and lowercase, with a related italic.

The plan was to combine the precision of a typeface such as Walbaum with the calligraphic energy of broad-edged pen letters in characters of condensed proportions. Capitals, ascenders and descenders were to be kept short, and serifs wide enough to discourage too close letter spacing. To achieve extra forward momentum vertical serifs were sloped, and all serifs thickened slightly at their

ends to increase definition. As usual the capitals were made slightly heavier in weight than the lowercase, and it was intended that the design should work easily in display and text settings.

Modern/broad-pen

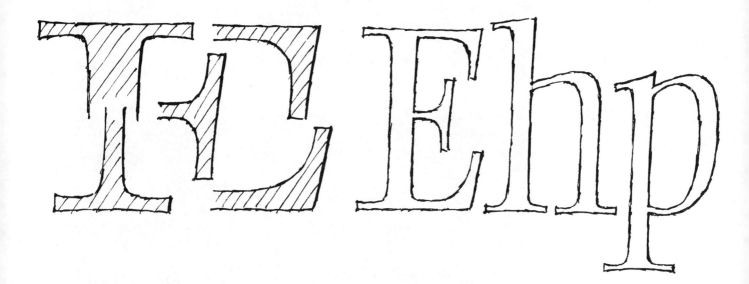

The condensed proportions affected the wider capitals (C, D, G, H, O and T) more than the narrower letters (B, E, F, K, L, P, R and S). Letters containing diagonals were only slightly narrowed to avoid thickening at junctions.

Tracing off from the common bases of n and o helped proportional consistency in the lowercase letters. Top serifs and arches of a, n, m and u were angled to give directional impetus, a feature also evident in the top curves of b and p, the lower curves of c, d, e, and q, and lower serifs of a, d, and u. While letters with diagonals follow the capital pattern, as do o and s, the tail of g is emphatically calligraphic. The dots of i and j were drawn as horizontally flattened ovals rather than round, a feature echoed in the rising ear of g and the tail of y.

ABCDE
FGHKM
RSTWZ

Using accurate guidelines, large drawings were made on detail paper thin
enough to be used on a lightbox. Fibre-
tipped pens, whose spirit-based inks dry
immediately and do not cause the paper
to wrinkle, are good for filling in the
outlines drawn with a fine technical pen.
It is better to work on groups of similar
letters, e.g., n h m, o c e, b p d q, than to
work through doggedly from a to z. When
an alphabet is completed, paste-up trial
words can be made with reduced photocopies. *Hamburgefonts* was made up in this
way using horizontal guidelines drawn
below each character as shown here and
which should be removed when the
word is fully assembled. At this stage in
the design process any shortcomings in
particular characters will become apparent and the original drawings may need
to be revised and further trials made.

Hamburgefonts

Italic faces are usually differentiated from roman by three factors, their slope, cursive quality and comparative narrowness. Here, because the roman was already narrow the first two factors were emphasised to maintain the difference between the faces.

Slope is normally slight in italic types that follow the original models from the sixteenth century. The Spectrum italic, designed in 1952, is modestly inclined at 9 degrees. In contrast eighteenth-century forms, such as Walbaum, lean forward at a steep angle of 16 degrees. Italic letters to accompany the roman shown on pages 114–115 were given a general slope of 12 degrees, but, as can be seen from the large drawings below, calligraphic liveliness required considerable departures from this norm.

Slightly more upright at 10 degrees, the capitals were drawn to complement the italic lowercase while retaining their essentially roman style, and, as with the roman alphabet, are shorter than the lowercase ascenders.

A comparison of the serifs of Spectrum and Walbaum shows the range of possibilities, sharply angular to smoothly round.

Spectrum 9°

Walbaum 16°

Lowercase 12°

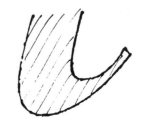

Capitals 10°

Spectrum

Walbaum

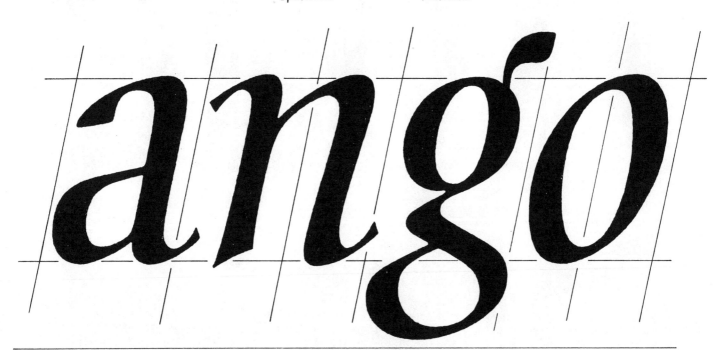

The serif designed for this italic followed broad-edged pen style by bringing the thickness around the bend, while being far less severe than Spectrum and less steeply upswept than Walbaum. The usual form of italic *a* was dropped in favour of the potentially more lively sloped roman lowercase character.

Trial paste-ups made from reduced photocopies are a quick way of assessing a design's virtues and shortcomings. Several words should be tried and modifications made, or alternatives drawn and experimented with, until the best possible fit of letters is achieved.

Explorations

Designing a typeface does not stop with the alphabet, for ligatures, figures, punctuation marks and characters such as ampersands will be required. Figures, originally Arabic, resist assimilation into roman type families and look best in the old style shown opposite in outline. The even height version (ranging) is best for use with capitals. A comprehensive typeface family will include both versions.

Italic alphabets require their own sloping figures, and in the design partly shown here the italic figure *8* is given a cursive treatment that is lacking in the upright figure.

The ampersand is a flexible character that can take various forms, particularly in italic. Other characters required to complete the family include exclamation and question marks, which should as far as possible follow the style set by the capital alphabet. Such ligatures as the fi shown here are essential if the disastrous overlapping of letters, which occurs in bad filmsetting, is to be avoided.

When all the characters are complete trial settings can be made to explore the design's potential. Here several arrangements are shown – large initials with smaller italics; large italic with roman capitals; lowercase with italic; a line of roman lowercase flanked with lines of small capitals; several lines of roman and italic lowercase in a large text size. These first trials may be pasted up from photocopies, carefully aligned with the aid of the guidelines drawn beneath each letter which are then removed, but if the design is to be used efficiently it must be converted from drawings to one of today's type production systems, of which dry transfer sheets and phototypesetting were once the main examples. Today, the computer offers the most flexible system (see pages 156–159).

Stewart **SE** *Editions*

Signal REVIEW

ABCDEFGHIJKLMNOPQRSTUVWXYZ
Methods of Book Design
ABCDEFGHIJKLMNOPQRSTUVWXYZ

Lettering letters drawn, inscribed, etc.
Drawing delineation with pencil or pen, etc., especially without colour; sketch.
Design plan, purpose; preliminary sketch or plan; general idea, construction, etc., faculty of evolving these; pattern.

English Opera *Festival*

All but two of this selection of type designs were photoset; Scorpio Script has not yet been produced and Zephyr was produced in hot metal. The type designed for the Tate Gallery, named Millbank, and that used for *Rebels & Rulers*, is closely related to the design described on pages 114–118. When a lot of hand lettering is required for a commission it can save time and eye-strain if an alphabet is drawn for use on a headline setting machine, or for paste-up. Both *The Birds of the Air* and *This little piggy . . .* were produced in this way, the first title for chapter headings and the other for a series of bookjackets.

Scorpio Script

THE BIRDS OF THE AIR

REBELS &RULERS

THE TATE GALLERY

This little piggy went to Market

Tate Gallery

ZEPHYR FOR BETTER ADS

3

Digital
letterforms

Equipment, tools and techniques

Although the equipment needed to produce digital characters is electronically sophisticated and expensive, it does simplify the lettering designer's work, particularly in the field of type design. The sketch below shows a typical designer's drawing board, several letter drawings (these need to be large and extremely accurate for type design purposes) and stacks of completed drawings. A typeface family of roman and italic in several weights may require upwards of one thousand such drawings, each needing to be easily accessible for reference and modification as the type's development proceeds.

In contrast the drawing opposite illustrates the smooth progress of a relatively small letter-drawing through a scanner, into the computer and onto the monitor where the scanned image appears as a large template. Once digitized on screen using the tools provided by the software, the character emerges from the laserprinter. The print is for evaluation purposes only: if anything is unsatisfactory the character can be edited on screen and further prints taken until the designer is satisfied. Existing only in digital form, every character, unlike its analogue predecessor, can be stored in the computer's memory or a backup floppy disk from where it can be instantly retrieved.

So the computer allows the designer to not only keep a tidy workspace but also provides control over every aspect of a design including, in a typeface, the spacing of characters, the almost instantaneous creation of extra weights in a family through interpolation, proportional variations and so on. Text can be set on screen to assess its qualities, removing a huge chore from designers who previously spent hours with scissors and gum assembling text by hand.

In this section it is not possible to give more than brief advice on equipment or the software that controls the digital processes, so it is assumed that

the reader is already familiar with the computer. If anything in this section is puzzling, the reader should read the appropriate manuals, those sometimes none-too-clear handbooks that every computer user has to live with.

My experience with the computer is based on a Macintosh with 8 megabytes of RAM (random access memory) linked to a 20 inch monochrome monitor. In a type designer's specialised work a colour monitor, which uses a lot of computer memory, is not necessary. A flat-bed scanner converts black and white drawings into templates and a 600 dpi (dots per inch) laser printer

provides test prints. The relatively high resolution output of the printer is essential for the exacting work of type design. Although only a few years old, my computer is already obsolete, but continues to work well. The large screen is excellent for designing typographic characters. A modem completes the equipment, enabling data to be sent anywhere in the world in a few minutes.

So much for hardware. The choice of software is less simple. Perversely, the program that I and some other type designers favour, FontStudio, is no longer available, but we stick to it because it is familiar and its interface is pleasantly intuitive. This is the reason why most of the illustrations on the following pages derive from that program. But the type design software called Fontographer is very similar in operation and uses the same Bézier curve principles to create outlines. Less specific computer graphics programs such as Adobe Illustrator, Macromedia Freehand and CorelDraw also use the Bézier curve system as the mathematical model for their much wider range of features. At least one professional type designer starts his designs in Illustrator because he is comfortable with its interface, then exports the results into FontStudio for continued development in that sophisticated typographic program. The other specialized type design software, Ikarus M, uses a digitizing tablet to digitize letters directly from drawings, but it is not discussed here.

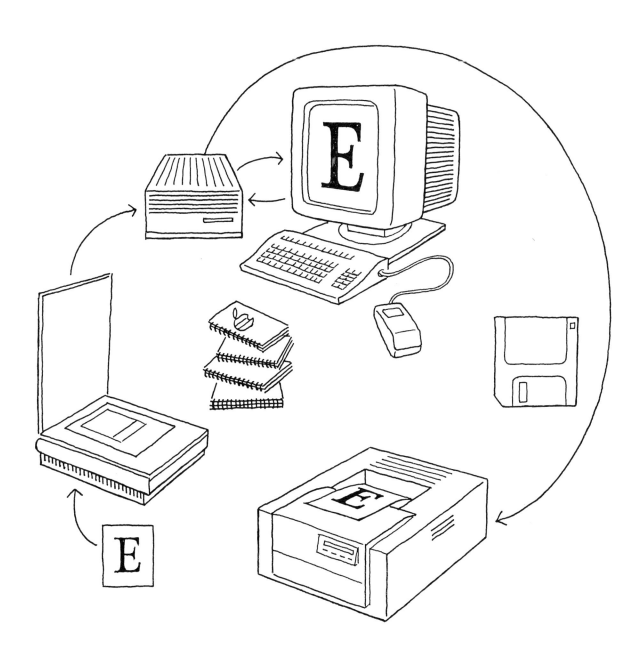

To one used to writing and drawing letters, the remote control of forms via keyboard and mouse can take some getting used to: a hands-off experience rather than hands-on. The direct shaping of letters in which the tactile feel of paper surface, ink and pen contribute to making a letter, bringing the mental image into being, is lost. The image on screen, which began as a drawing, even though it is now a digital outline, can still be judged in the light of previous experience in the making of 'analogue' letters. For this reason it is essential to bring some of that experience to the computer screen, and why it is foolish to try to manipulate existing typefaces on screen without the understanding of letterforms that comes from making them by hand. The distorted and senseless lettering sometimes used in advertising campaigns today, trying so hard to be creative, comes from such ignorance.

With practice, the remoteness of screen, keyboard and mouse lessens, and the computer becomes just another tool. If we know what we want we can soon learn to coax this powerful tool into coming up with the goods.

The screen image is large and can be

fi	alt/opt	shift	5
fl	alt/opt	shift	6
æ	alt/opt	'	
Æ	alt/opt	shift	'
œ	alt/opt	q	
Œ	alt/opt	shift	q
'	alt/opt	]	
"	alt/opt	[	
'	alt/opt	shift	]
,,	alt/opt	shift	[

magnified further to bring details into sharp focus. The mouse directs the pointer and the various 'tools' (hand-craft terms survive reassuringly in the computer environment) with which we create and manipulate the screen image, clicking and double-clicking as we go. The keyboard offers shortcuts that allow the mouse to rest, and gives access to other characters such as those shown at right. The extended Macintosh keyboard includes 'undo', 'cut', 'copy' and 'paste' keys that further speed up operations. In practice only a few keys are regularly used by most designers of on-screen letters: 'command (Apple)-A' to select all of an image, 'command-X' to delete and, perhaps the most important of all, 'command-S' to save the work just completed.

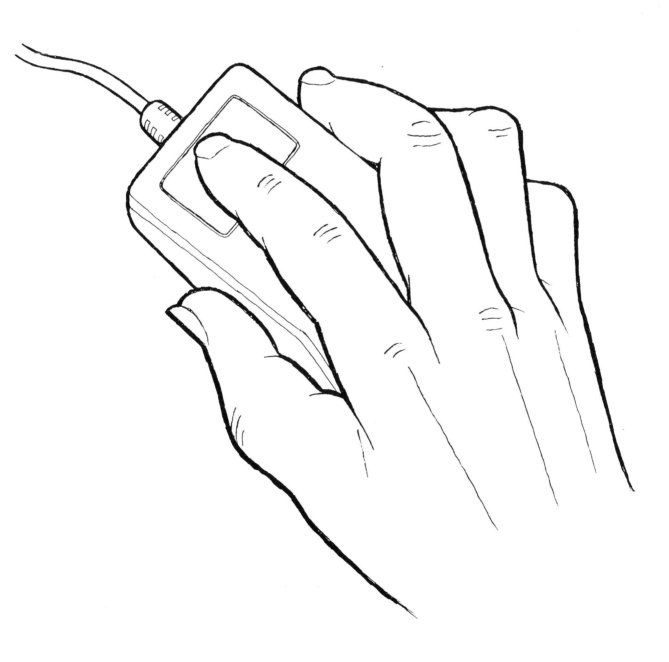

Software tools

The tool icons, shown here divided into groups, come from various software programs but readers will easily be able to relate them to whichever program they are using. As always, it is important to become familiar with the software man-ual. All the tool functions and particular ways of working will be found there, and when things go wrong the manual is the first place to look for help. Here it is only possible to describe tools and their functions in very general terms.

Pointer

The mouse guides the pointer or cur-sor, selects tools and functions and con-trols much of the action on screen; clicking, double-clicking, and dragging the Bézier control points.

Image making

The top line of this group includes a hand that when selected by the pointer moves images and templates around the character window, and three drawing tools, the pen being the one used for digitizing outlines, and a tool that simu-lates broad-edged pen writing. In the second line is a freehand drawing tool and three point-selection tools – curve, corner and tangent – from the Fontog-rapher program. The paint bucket tool is in the third line. Selecting this fills an outline image solid black in some pro-grams.

Enlarging and measuring

The magnifying glass enlarges in per-centage steps, and, in most programs with the 'alt/opt' key depressed, reduces the image. Tape and ruler give accurate linear measurements.

Path cutting

Fontographer's knife cuts paths, while FontStudio's scissors can also add points. Paths are cut to allow, for instance, parts of letters to be removed and brought together to make ligatures, such as æ.

Image altering

This group includes tools for sloping the image, flipping it over vertically or horizontally, rotating (an upside-down view of a character will often help locate any faults) resizing and scaling.

Library

Here is where lazy designers store repeated letter parts such a serifs, to be retrieved and bolted on as required.

Below is a typical outline font window. It contains 256 spaces in its grid, allowing for capitals, lowercase, numerals, punctuation, ligatures, accented characters, currency symbols, mathematical symbols, foreign language characters and the other assorted characters and symbols that make up a typeface family. Type design is a protracted business and its complexity can be likened to writing a symphony or a long book or play teeming with characters. Each character can be selected with the pointer tool and the character window opened up. Each new family the designer creates must be named and defined (light, bold, italic, etc.). Naturally the designer will ensure against computer crashes by making backup copies on floppy disks, keeping one in a separate location to be safe. Loss of hours (or days) of work can be avoided by this simple precaution, which, to the experienced computer worker, becomes second nature.

The font window is the digital equivalent of the type case in which metal type was distributed in the days when type was set by hand. Such a case is shown at the foot of the page, its irregular divisions allowing more space for the most commonly used characters.

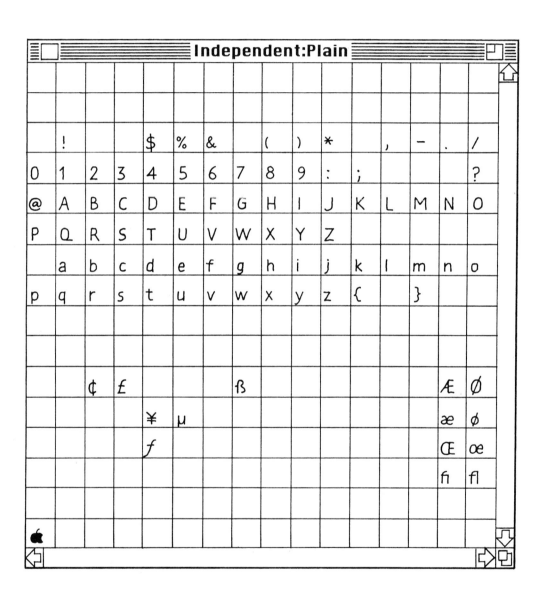

Bitmaps and Bézier curves

Bitmaps

Bitmaps consist of tiny dots called pixels that produce both the screen image and a laser printer's output. The relative crudity of bitmaps is evident in this letter A: its outline is smooth but the building blocks of the bitmap have difficulty following the diagonals, and the swelling terminals are impossible to define successfully. In this enlarged example the hit-and-miss effect is very apparent, but in small sizes may be less noticeable. The more pixels a bitmap has in a given area the finer the image will be. This resolution or image quality is tied to the output device, so is ultimately beyond the designer's control, although letters can be designed specifically for low resolution output. The three As below show the effects of different resolutions.

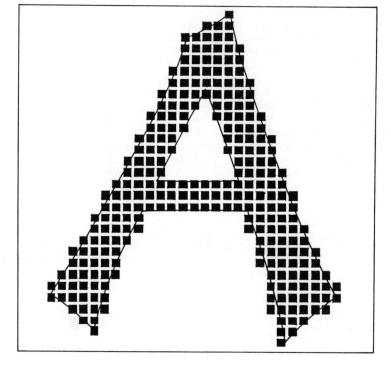

Bézier curves

The outlines drawn by the designer on screen are a representation of mathematically generated curves, defined by anchor or end points, and guide or control points (BCPs or Bézier Control Points in Fontographer, named after their inventor Pierre Bézier). These basic elements are shown to right, a round end point (curve) and a square end point (corner), both with two control points at the end of straight handles.

These illustrations, arranged in three columns, show stages in manipulating segments (the line between two end points). In the first column a straight segment is followed by a two-segment line in which the central point has been placed to make an angle, while below control points have been dragged to make the line into an arch. Solid arrows indicate the general direction of the digitizing movement, and the dotted arrows the direction in which control points have been dragged.

In the middle column, dragging the control points upwards has created a symmetrical curve, then an asymmetrical curve has been made by dragging the lefthand control point down. In the lower example, the form of the curve is controlled with an additional endpoint (this is now a two-segment path) and its control points.

The last column shows the previous examples altered by further extension of the control points.

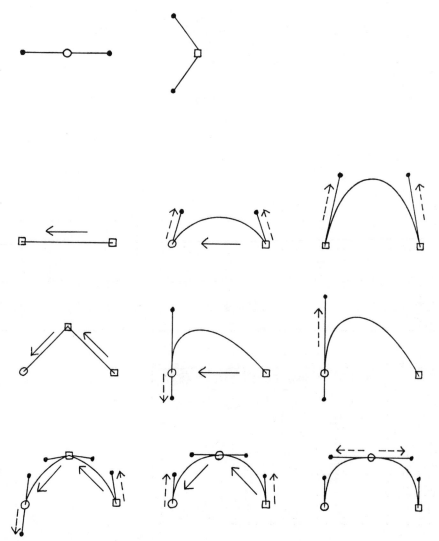

The illustration at right shows four variations on a serpentine double curve of three segments and four end points. Two inner points have tangental extended control points, and those at each end have single control points. In the second variation (far right) the end points have been moved further apart along the horizontal axis, changing the shape of the curve. Below, this process has been continued to produce an even wider double curve. The final example modulates the line further by reducing the vertical distance between the inner points. In each variation the handles of the control points have been dragged with the pointer tool to maintain smoothness in the curves.

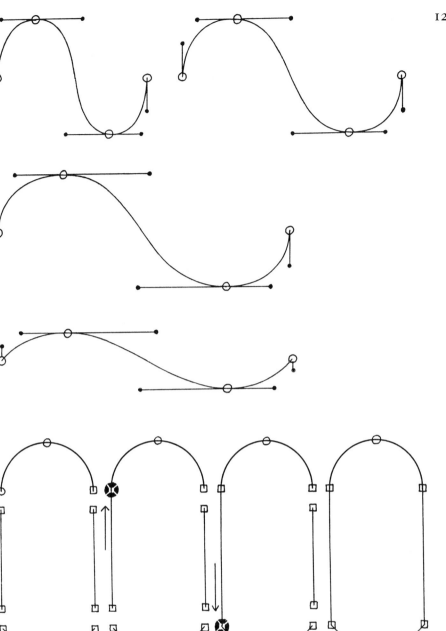

Segments and paths

The outlines of a digital letter are built from segments which connect to make a path; when the first and last end points meet the path is closed. Basic segments are shown at right as curved, straight and corner elements. Depending on the software in use end points may be square (for corners), round (for curves) or, in Fontographer, triangular (where straights meet curves). Only round and square end points are shown in this illustration.

To create a path, segments have to be joined, a process that can be followed here, the open end points of the left-hand straight being moved vertically to meet the corresponding open end points above and below. When the righthand straight is similarly connected a closed path results.

All extremes in a path should be given an end point, and their control points must be aligned horizontally or vertically, as shown in this lowercase letter. The novice easily forgets this.

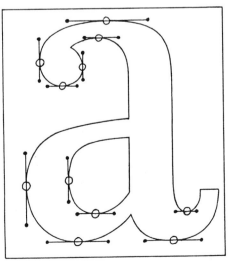

Letters for scanning

Type designers often start with small sketches to be certain that the weights and proportions are right at working sizes, then work on enlargements to refine forms. My method is similar, as described below, but some experienced designers work directly on screen without preliminary drawings.

A roman family

The outline drawings here are taken from enlarged photocopies of sketches like those above, using guidelines and careful measurement to ensure accuracy.

Filled in black, each letter is enlarged on a photocopier to the size below. It is a good policy at this time to rule a baseline between each letter, a useful check that the scan is straight when it appears as a template on screen, and another on the reverse to help alignment when the drawing is placed face down on the bed of the scanner. Set the scanner to enlarge the drawing to give a template that is comfortable to work with. Each letter is individually scanned, saved in either *Pict* or *Tiff* format, whichever the software requires, and placed in a scan file ready to be called up into the relevant character window for digitizing. Name the scan, distinguishing between capitals and lowercase.

ABCDEFGHIJ

ABCDEFGHI

Light/bold extremes

To automatically generate intermediate weights, both light and bold master fonts are required. The drawing of a light design can be used to trace the left side, shifted, then trace the right side to create a bold version, as in these examples. In this way a certain consistency and family look is maintained. Care at this stage is important too if good interpolations (see page 146) are to result, and attention to these early stages on the drawing board will save much time in making on-screen adjustments later.

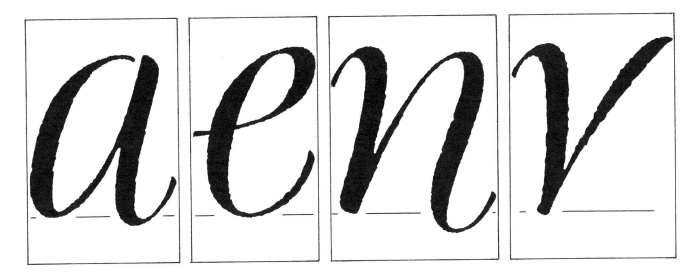

Script forms

The designer of a script-based typeface, especially if it is to be an informal design, may write out characters several times (see also page 46) before selecting the best letters for scanning. In the editing process the pen's thinner hairlines may need strengthening before scanning (or on screen later), a precaution that will avoid disappointment when the type is tested in small sizes. Rough edges may be kept, but at the expense of much extra work on screen carefully placing the extra points; the final typeface will also consume more memory.

Digitizing outline characters

Open the program either by double-clicking on its icon or that of the family already created (page 127). Double-click a character in the font window to open up its character window. This will show a baseline intersected by a vertical at the point of intersection to mark the character's origin. A toolbox will also appear and a place where digital read-outs will be displayed (see page 136).

Now is the time to set certain software options (File, menu bar). Choose to make backups and set the number of 'undos' to at least 20 – it may be necessary to return several steps to an earlier version of a letter. Check to see that any 'snap to' commands are turned off. These automatic features are often a hindrance to a creative designer.

Before digitizing can begin, the letter's scan – its original appears below –

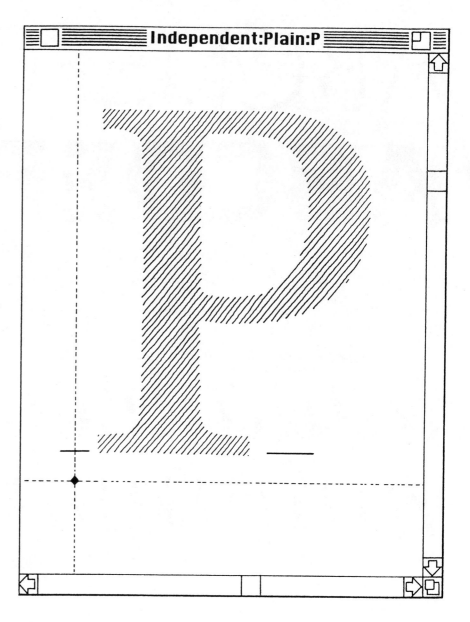

Independent:Plain:P

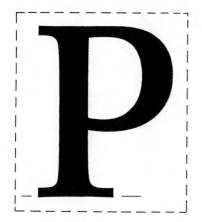

must be displayed in the window to act as a template (command-T). This should have been named when it was saved. If scans are not named correctly, access will be less convenient. The template that appears will have to be dragged into position with the hand tool, then a top guide line can be added to determine the height of the character. (Fontographer provides a separate layer for guide lines).

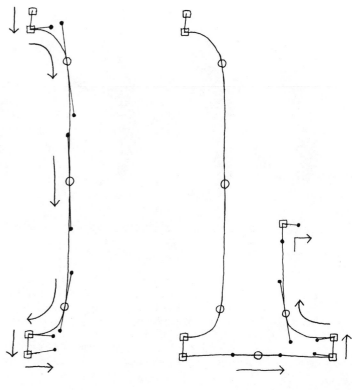

The digitizing process can now begin. Select the pen tool and guide it to a convenient starting place on the edge of the scan, as in the first illustration below left. Release the mouse and the first end point appears. Moving anti-clockwise, continue to place end points, dragging out control points before releasing the mouse button. Select the correct kind of end point for each position (see page 126). As the mouse drags each control point a Bézier segment will appear connecting the new end point to the previous one. Accuracy is not important at this stage: points can be moved later at the editing stage, but use as few points as possible to describe the form.

Proceed around the character, following the sequence shown below, placing points until the first point is reached and the path is closed. Before digitizing the inner path deselect the pen tool briefly or else the inner and outer paths will be joined. Now, this time moving in a clockwise direction, digitize the inner path, beginning in the top left corner (fourth stage in sequence below). In most programs it is important that, in characters with enclosed spaces, inner and outer paths move in opposite directions. Save your work.

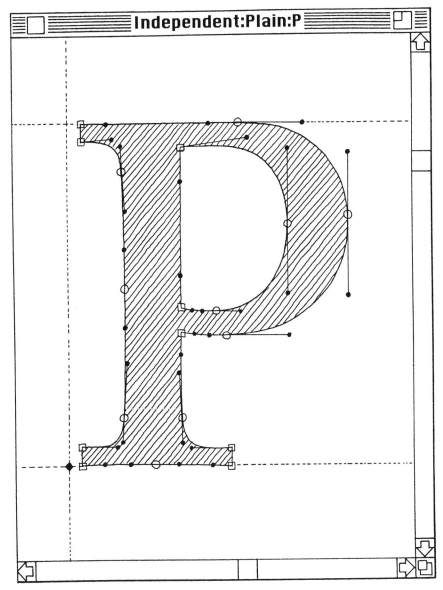

Independent:Plain:P

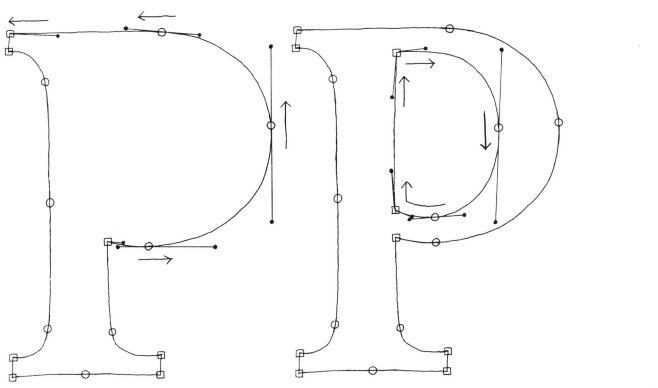

Fine tuning

One big advantage of digital over hand-drawn letters is that re-touching with ink and white paint is replaced by easing control points until the desired form is achieved. Either the mouse or the keyboard's directional keys are used, holding down the shift key to constrain movement to the vertical or horizontal. When the points are hidden – a click of the mouse in FontStudio, a keyboard command in Fontographer – just the outline is left, and with the template hidden too the letter is seen uncluttered for the first time: an exciting moment. During this process the outline can be filled (see page 138) to allow the form to be judged more easily.

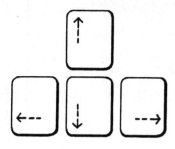

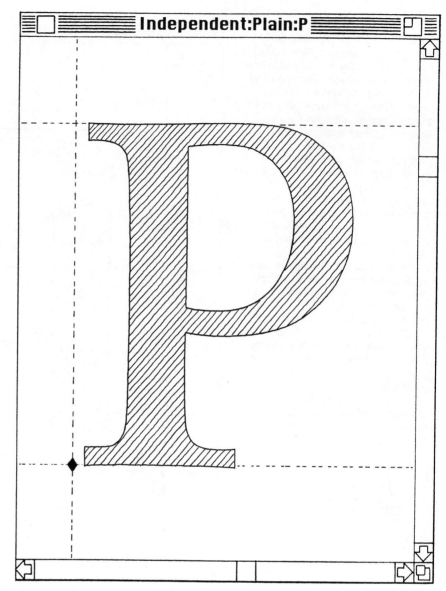

Independent:Plain:P

Adding and deleting points

When a curve refuses to respond to the fine-tuning process, remaining stubbornly lumpy, extra points may need to be added to improve control in that area. The tools that do this vary from one program to another. Curiously, the scissors tool in FontStudio performs this task. Two areas where an extra point can help are shown in the letter on the right, the one on the inner path a necessary point overlooked in the initial digitization. These little touches that keep a line from appearing too symmetrical or mechanical may make all the difference.

Sometimes it is possible to get away with fewer points once the form has been fine-tuned. These are usually intermediate points in a curve's path and can be removed with keyboard commands, but if the form suffers, replace them ('undo' in the File menu). In general, the fewer points in each character the less memory storage will be needed for the final font.

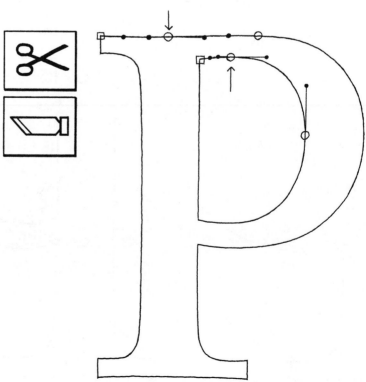

Magnification

The ability to get in really close is another advantage the digital designer has over the draftsman. Using the magnifying tool, selected details can be greatly enlarged in an instant, allowing the designer to see clearly when making very fine adjustments, then, with the 'option/alt' key held down, to return the image as speedily to its normal screen size. It is also possible to vary the image size using keyboard commands or going to the menu bar to select a particular enlargement or reduction.

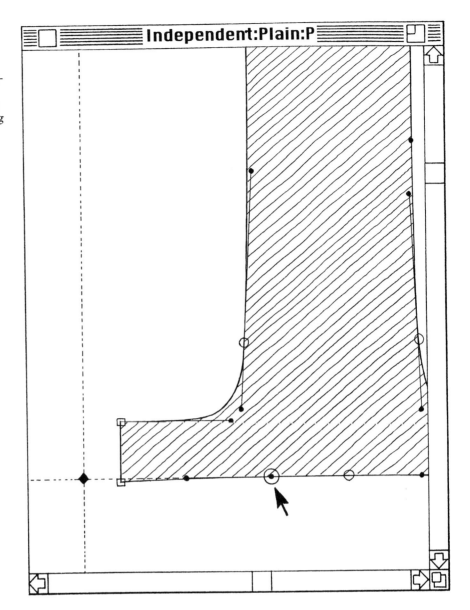

Points at extremes

Check now that all extreme points are vertical or horizontal (see page 129). The illustration here shows, on the left, incorrectly aligned control points and, on the right, how they should be aligned. This principle is evident in many other examples in these pages.

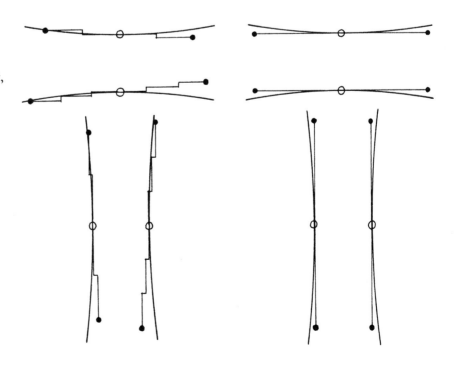

Readouts

Another advantage of the digital process is that accuracy and consistency throughout a type family is easily achieved, by referring to the readouts at top of the character window, where the exact position of each selected point is displayed. These x and y co-ordinates offer a precise method of checking, for example, that all serifs are the same weight or that all similar stems have the same width.

In the letter at right, each point in the outer path is numbered and their x and y co-ordinates are given in the chart below. Along the bottom of these pages are letters whose points share the same positions on the digital grid. The type designer values these aids to quality control, even though absolute conformity may often be over-ridden to avoid sterility in a design.

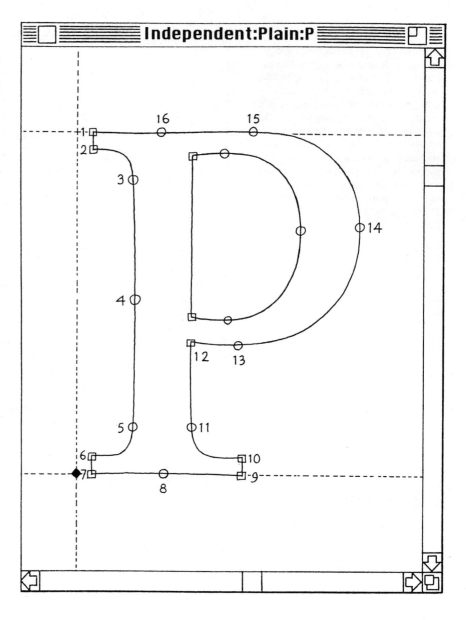

	X	y
1	25	565
2	25	533
3	93	493
4	97	297
5	94	73
6	25	29
7	25	-3
8	144	0
9	284	-3
10	284	29
11	197	77
12	194	219
13	273	213
14	482	407
15	292	565
16	140	564

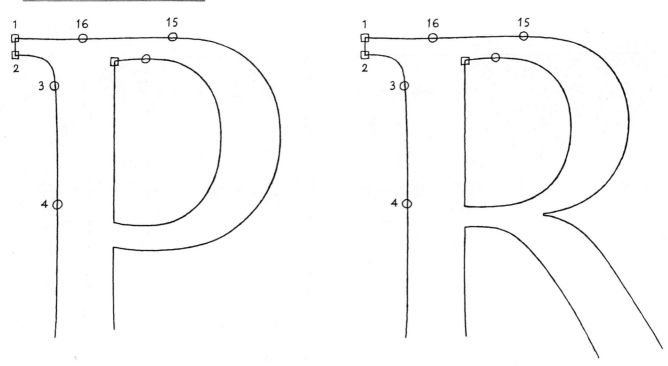

Measuring

A simple way to check dimensions, a carry-over from the days of drawing board and ruler, is the measuring tool the software provides, and the Macintosh's on-screen calculator (or an external model) is another way of checking the linear dimensions of characters and strokes. Once the widths are known for one letter or stem, these values can be applied to other similar letters in the family.

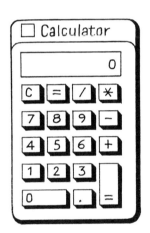

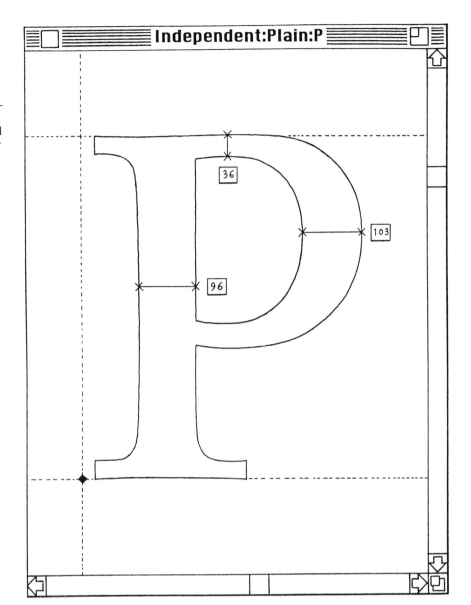

Independent:Plain:P

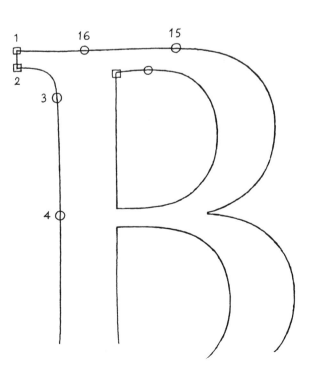

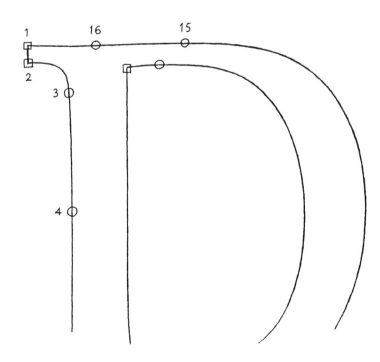

138 Sidebearings

Although the character has been digitized it does not really exist in its own space until given a body width. The lefthand vertical boundary of this invisible body is already in place but now the righthand boundary has to be fixed with a second vertical. The manual will explain how this is done. The sidebearings, as the spaces between the character and the sides of its body are known, are usually approximate at first. The proper letterspacing (or letterfit) is worked out later (page 156) when enough characters have been digitized to set the spacing between them.

Filling in

So far the digital letters shown on these pages have appeared as a white space inside an outline, but to judge a letter's real appearance it must be filled in black. Selecting the paint bucket from the toolbox does this in some programs (Fontographer uses the keyboard commands shown below, hiding the points and making the letter solid). A designer will spend some time switching back and forth from outline to solid, making small adjustments until the letter passes muster.

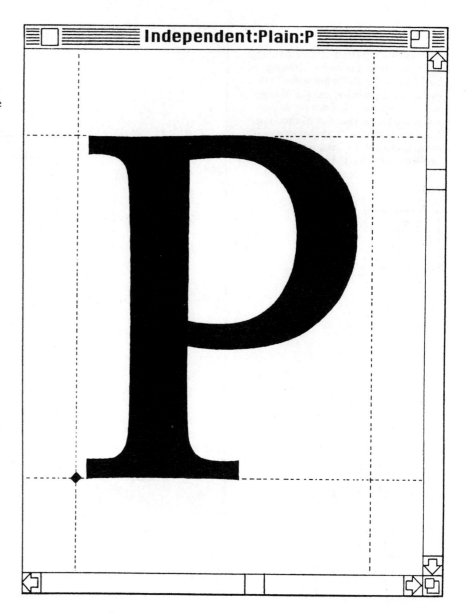

Jaggies

The pixels that make up the black-filled screen image produce rough edges at low resolutions, as explained on page 128, and letters on a monitor screen are very low resolution indeed. The designer learns to ignore this apparent crudeness of image, these jaggies, and for real evidence of a character's merits turns to laser prints and high resolution output.

Printing

The printed image brings the digital letter out of the computer and into the real world. Each character can be printed as an outline, showing the position of its points (plus digital 'readout' data), or as a solid black shape. Now any irregularities, lumpy curves and other flaws that the screen's low resolution failed to display become apparent. With a marked-up print as a guide the screen character can be worked on and further prints taken until the result matches the designer's intention, the idea that began with the drawing made at the start of the process.

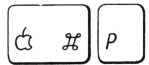

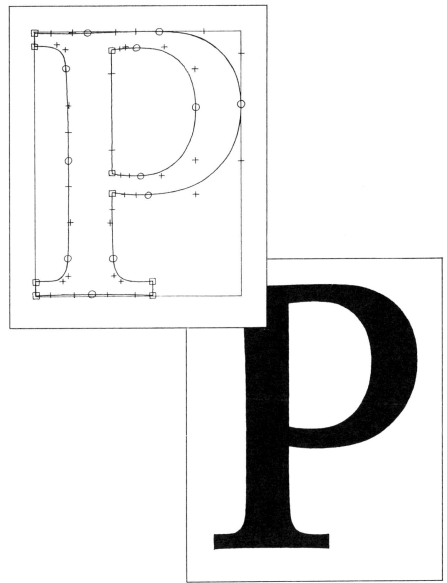

Assorted sizes

Fontographer's program allows each letter to be printed out in a range of sizes, a useful guide to how a design performs at the small end of its range where optical factors, such as weight loss and clogged counter shapes, become evident.

Each design may be proofed at a variety of resolutions – 72, 300, 600 and 1200 dpi – and across the size range at which it is intended to be used: 6 to 24pt for a text typeface, 18 to 72 for a display design.

P P P P P P

P P P P P P P P P P P P P

Complex forms

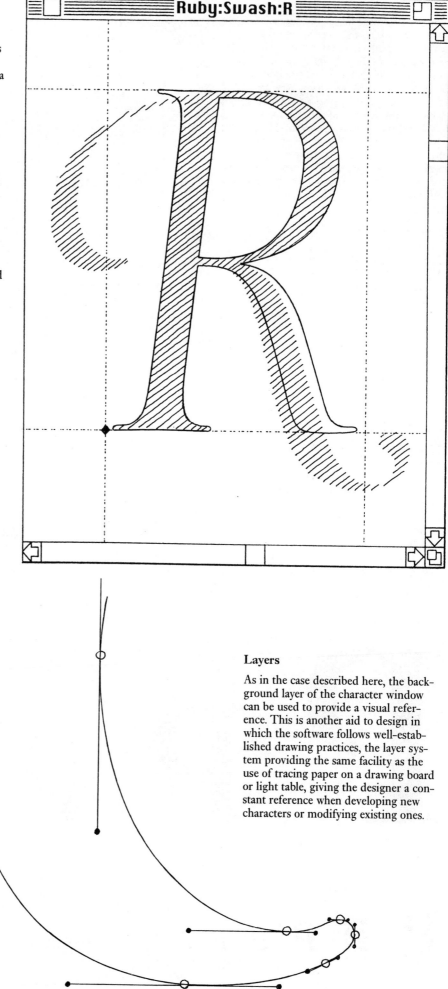

A swash letter with sweeping flourishes requires careful point placement to obtain a faithful digital rendering with a calligraphic verve. Where a designer might use french curves as a guide when drawing these curvilinear lines, capturing them in digital form must be done by eye alone. The Bézier curve offers countless possibilities, but time and patience are needed to find the optimum placement of end and control points.

In the window at right an italic capital R is shown, with a template of the swash version in the background. This copy of the existing R has been placed into this character window so that its outline can be stretched and augmented to fit the template. On the opposite page the process is complete, the ghost of the original letter in the background layer where it acts as a control image. The tail of the swash letter has a steeper angle to allow the flourish the room it needs.

Below, enlarged details show the placement of points on both flourishes: note the extra points between the extremes to control the curves in some situations.

Ruby:Swash:R

Layers

As in the case described here, the background layer of the character window can be used to provide a visual reference. This is another aid to design in which the software follows well-established drawing practices, the layer system providing the same facility as the use of tracing paper on a drawing board or light table, giving the designer a constant reference when developing new characters or modifying existing ones.

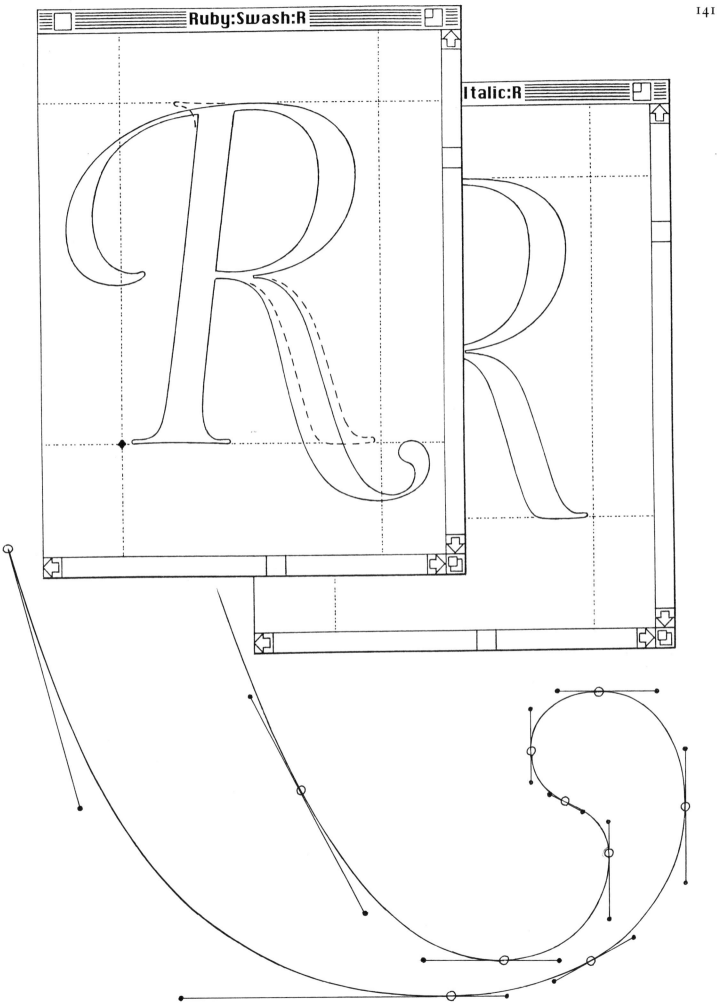

Building from parts

It is tempting to use the computer's facility to copy and paste virtually instantaneously, to take parts of letters and with them construct new characters on screen. Everyone uses these shortcuts sometimes, a practice among designers going back to the days of cutting up photocopies and reassembling them to make composite letters. The computer simply makes this a much speedier operation, but then as now the forms arrived at will need careful scrutiny. Although each stem or serif may look the same this is no guarantee that they will work in other situations without minuscule changes.

With that warning in mind, the illustrations here show some possible letter constructions, the simplest, right, a capital H made from two Is copied and pasted side by side. Their outlines cut, (with knife or scissors tool), the Is are then joined horizontally with the pen tool.

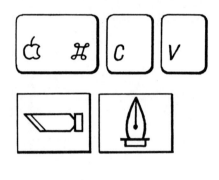

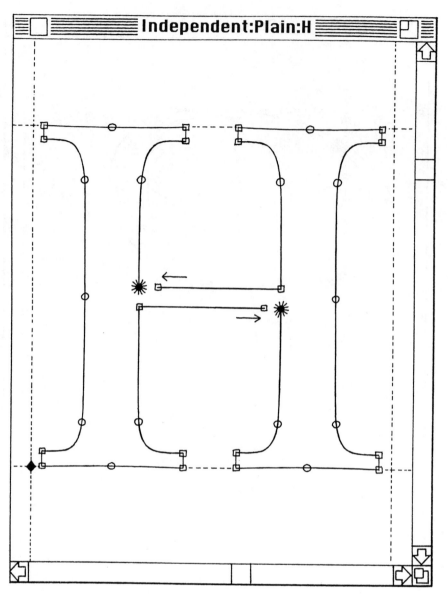

Developing a repeated form

Lowercase letters have several similar parts, such as the arched form that occurs in h, n, m and u, which are obvious candidates for copy-and-paste design work. Here the n is the h with the ascender shortened by selecting the top serif and pulling it down with the mouse, while constraining sideways movement. The n and its arch have been copied side by side in the m window, while the u is an n rotated through 180 degrees with new serifs added at the top. Both m and u should be narrowed slightly. Always check that serifs have the correct angle in their new position.

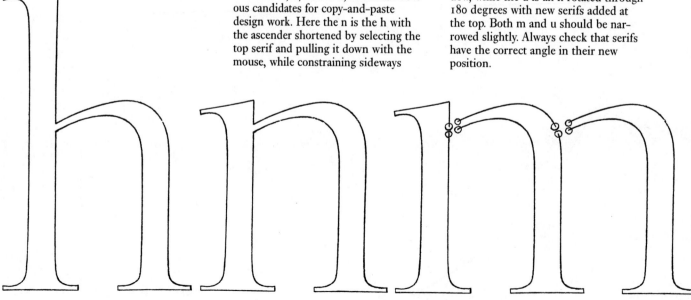

Italic lowercase has even more forms in common and, as these examples show, the basic *a* form can be copied and pasted to form the bowl of *d* and *q* and rotated through 180 degrees to make the basis of *b* and *p*. Ascenders and descenders can be copied from other characters

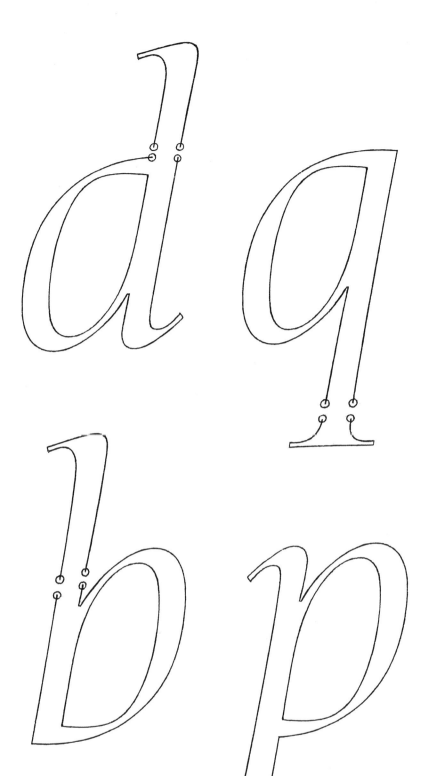

and bolted on. Again, these composites should not be left as they stand. The outlines so quickly made will have to be examined and edited sympathetically if convincing letters are to be achieved.

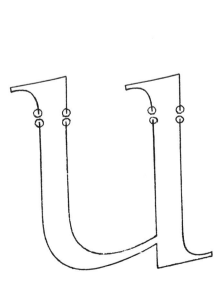

A library of parts

This is an easy way to store often-repeated elements such as serifs, but do not assume that they will work in every situation without adjustment.

Making a bold weight

The powerful interpolation facilities of sophisticated type design software encourages the design of whole families of type. To create extra weights two master fonts are required for the interpolation to take place. With a light weight letter already digitized and copied into the corresponding bold's character window, it is quite simple to make a bold character, stretching the light version to fit the bold template previously scanned from a drawn letter, avoiding going through the digitizing process a second time. In this way, as well as saving time, both weights will have the same points in approximately the same places on their outlines, which is necessary for a successful interpolation.

On the right a character window holds the light A, and far right the same letter's outline copied (command C, command V) into the bold window over a bold template, placed so that the left edges coincide. The sequence below shows the transformation from light to bold.

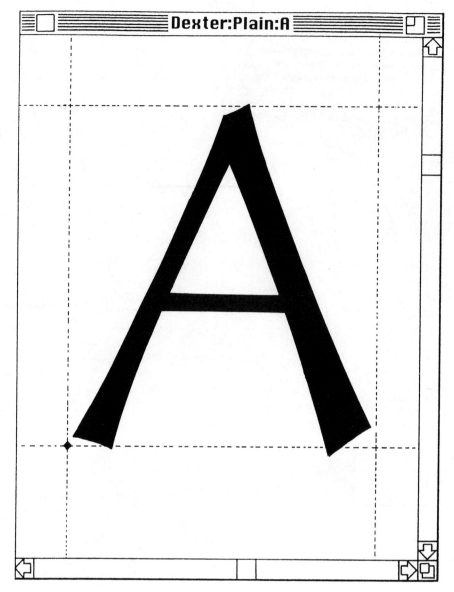

With the outer segment of the righthand diagonal's path selected, it is dragged by the pointer tool to the edge of the template.

The inner segment of the righthand diagonal's path is selected and pushed to the left by the pointer tool until it fits the edge of the template.

The point of the inner apex is selected and dragged down until it fits the corresponding apex on the template.

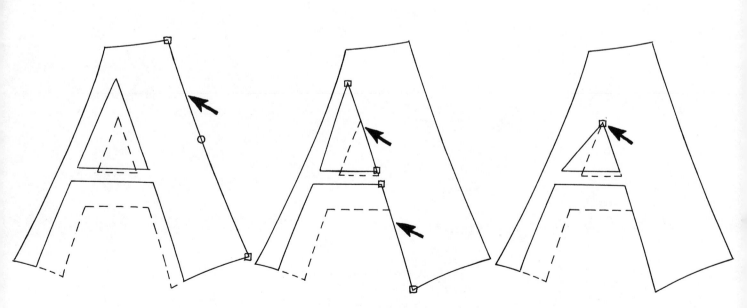

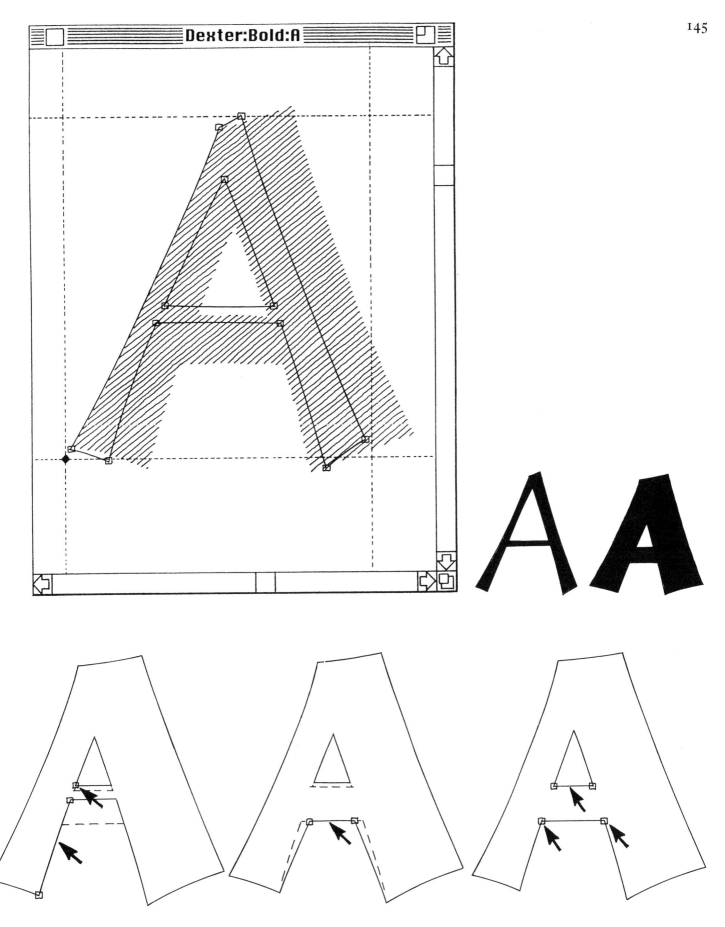

Dexter:Bold:A

The point below the apex is selected and dragged to the template's inner edge, followed by the lower segment.

The lower segment of the bar is selected and dragged down, leaving its points clear of the template.

The upper segment is selected and dragged down and the points of the lower segment moved horizontally to fit the template. Fine-tuning follows.

Interpolation

For interpolation of additional weights
between the extremes, light and bold,
two masters must be meticulously prepared, their paths going in the same
direction and the same number and
types of points in approximately the
same positions. These master characters
are shown in the windows at right and
opposite. Creating the bold master as
described on page 144 will help ensure
that these conditions are met.

Interpolation is only possible using
one of the dedicated type design programs such as FontStudio or Fontographer, each with its own procedure
described in the manual. The designer
chooses a new weight by percentage. If
the light font is 0% and the bold font
100%, 33% will generate a medium
font and 66% a bold letter that is not as
heavy as the bold master, which might
now be renamed 'extra bold'. The
results of these percentages are shown
below and it will be seen that the paths
are complete with points, enabling the
outlines to be modified if required.
Each will have its own character window and can be accessed just like the
master fonts. So from a single digitized
character three more weights have been
created, two without the designer doing
more than make choices. Many more
weights could be made to suit particular needs, the process being akin to the
two-axis multiple master typeface
described on pages 148 and 149.

A word of warning. Always work
with copies of the master fonts just in
case they become corrupted during the
interpolation process.

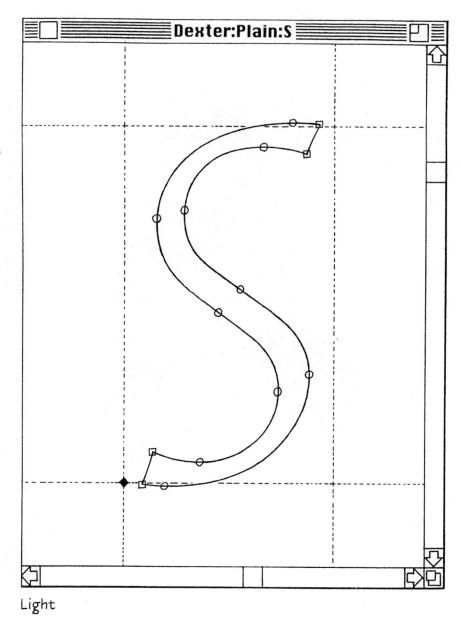

Dexter:Plain:S

Light

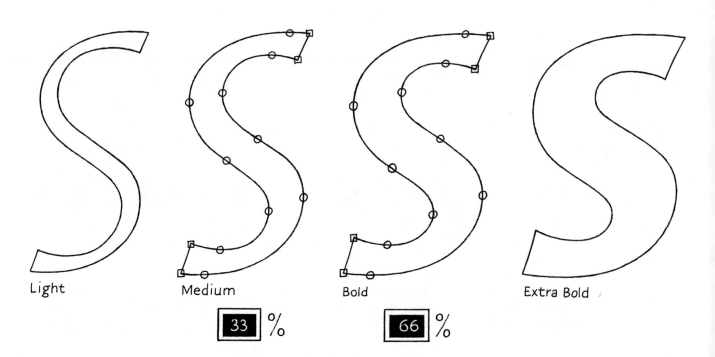

Light   Medium   Bold   Extra Bold

33 %   66 %

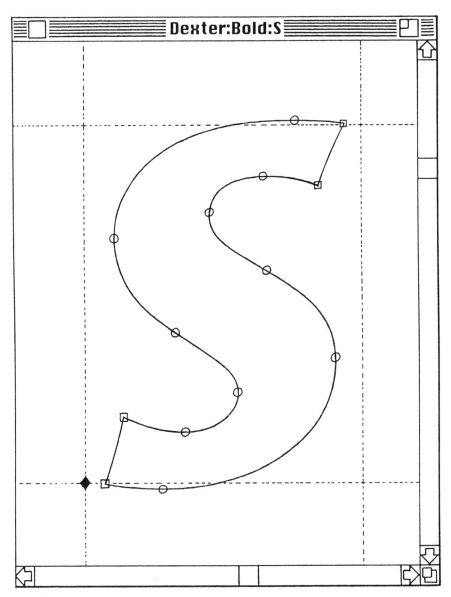

Bold

Fried characters

Sometimes interpolation is unsuccessful and spectacular 'fried' characters can result. When this happens, check that the masters are compatible, see if the points match (maybe a point is hidden by another stray point or the path is broken) and try again.

Unwanted points

Interpolated characters may acquire extra, unwanted points, mysteriously added during the process. These can be edited out, a small chore considering that the character was created in a matter of seconds.

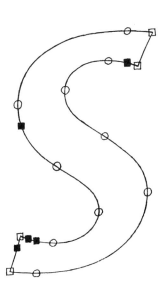

Dexter:Plain:Cond:R

Light condensed

Dexter:Bold:Cond:R

Bold condensed

Multiple master typefaces

Multiple master technology, developed by Adobe Systems, can provide the user with an extremely wide choice of variations within a single typeface design. Interpolation is at the heart of this phenomenon, which, as well as allowing the user to generate any weight between two extremes (single axis) may also vary proportions of width (two axis), generate designs optimized for specific sizes (three axis) and blend styles (four axis). A four-axis multiple master typeface in which all variations interact requires sixteen master designs, the maximum the technology can currently handle. In practical terms it is now possible to choose a particular proportion, weight, style and optical size that will meet exactly a graphic designer's typographic needs.

Due to its complexity, it is usual for designs to be developed by manufac-

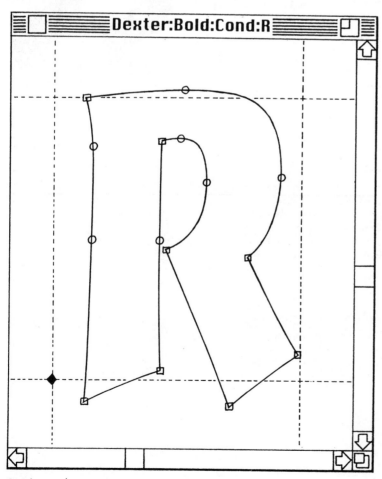

turer's in-house designers or by individuals collaborating with the manufacturer.

A two-axis multiple master typeface requires four master fonts: light condensed, bold condensed, light expanded and bold expanded, represented here by the Rs in the four character windows Because the type designer has carefully tuned the master fonts, the kinds of distortion that are described on pages 152 and 153 will be avoided throughout the whole range of font variations. This was a major consideration behind the development of multiple master technology.

Fontographer is the only commercially available software that allows the designer to generate a multiple master typeface unaided, but the manual warns of the many attempts that may be needed to make a successful design.

The illustration below shows some of the variety of letters possible with a two-axis multiple master font. Imagine all the other letter variations that lie unseen and you will have some idea of the enormous dynamic range offered to the designer by multiple master technology.

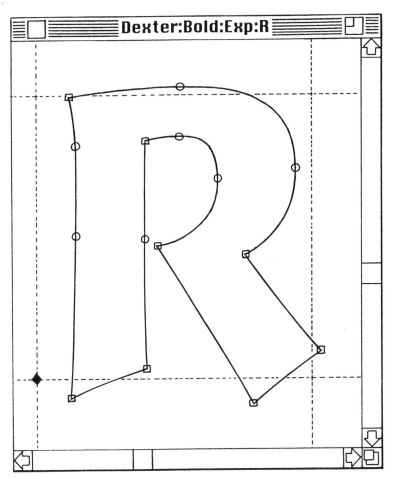

Bold expanded

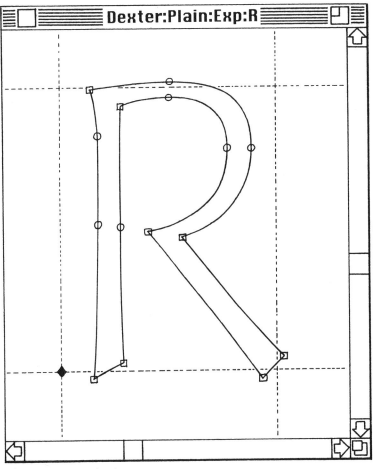

Light expanded

150   Optical scaling

Multiple master typefaces can provide 'optical scaling', characters becoming progressively bolder as they reduce in size. When type was made by hand and each size individually designed, the smaller sizes were often considerably strengthened to increase their legibility, but until multiple master technology reinstated this practice in digital type one master had to do for both display and text, which resulted in small sizes often appearing too light, an effect linked to the fact that area diminishes by twice the amount of linear reduction. Now, with optical scaling each size can be given optimum weight, sidebearings and other enhancement for increased legibility.

In the example, below the lefthand column shows letters from a single master diminishing in size. Notice how under-weight the smaller sizes look, then compare these with those in the other column where optical scaling produces satisfactory letters at each size. The slight but significant increases in weight and width are evident in the lower of the outline masters shown at right.

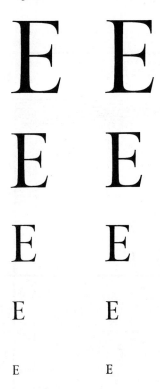

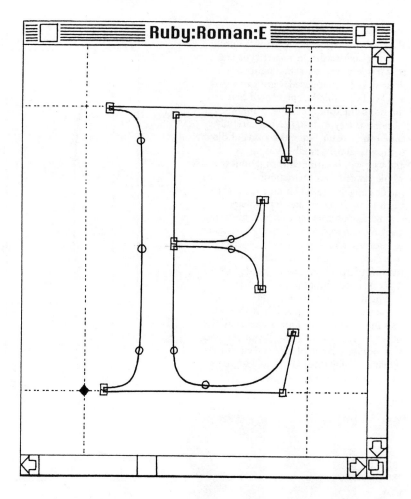

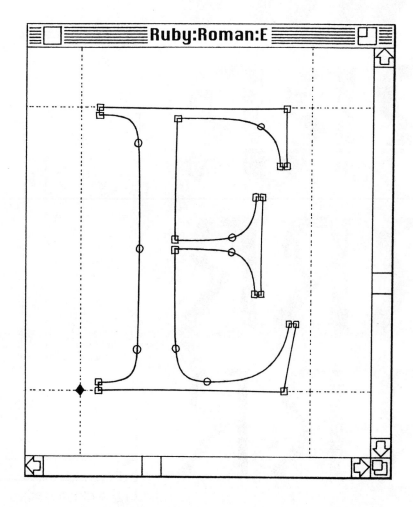

Blending styles

Letters from two master fonts, one a roman seriffed form, the other a plain sanserif, are shown, at right, while some of their hybrid off-spring appear below. Adding style-blending to other multiple master-generated ranges produces the widest possible variety within a single package. At the time of writing this is relatively unexplored territory. Possibilities include blending pointed and square serif fonts or different script styles; there is much fertile ground lying between the main letter styles waiting to be explored in this way, just as long as the results have a use and are not a gimmick.

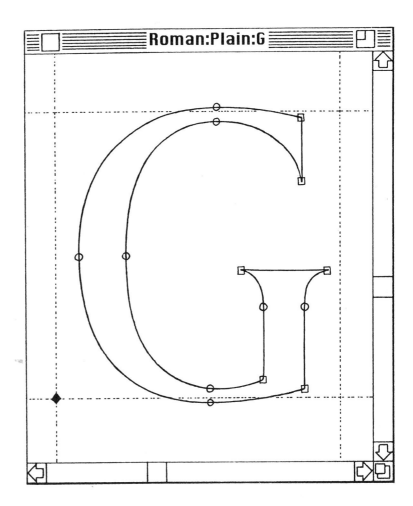

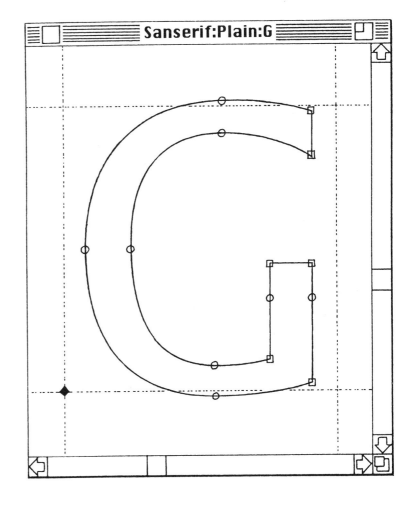

Digital variations

It is not necessary to use multiple master programs to alter such fundamentals as proportion, slope and weight: these changes can easily be made to individual characters on-screen.

Proportion

The points in an outline path can be moved closer or further apart vertically or horizontally. By typing a chosen percentage of scale in a dialogue box all the points will move and a new image will appear. In the examples here, where a reduction to 70% on the horizontal axis has produced condensed versions of E and S, the original forms remaining in the background. But notice the distortions that occur (a common sight in mechanically condensed type). In E the main vertical is now too thin, unlike the

arms which were less affected by the transformation. To bring the inner vertical back to its original position is a simple task, following the original letter in the background layer. The S is more difficult to rescue from its distorted condition. The thinner parts of the top left and lower right curves are now too light, but moving the inner points of both right and left respectively will make a big improvement. Then the points controlling the central sweep will need moving up and down respectively to restore weight. Much fine-tuning is needed to achieve a satisfactory letter. Above, the unedited letters are shown on the left beside the corrected forms. Note that these narrower letters will also need to have their character widths adjusted.

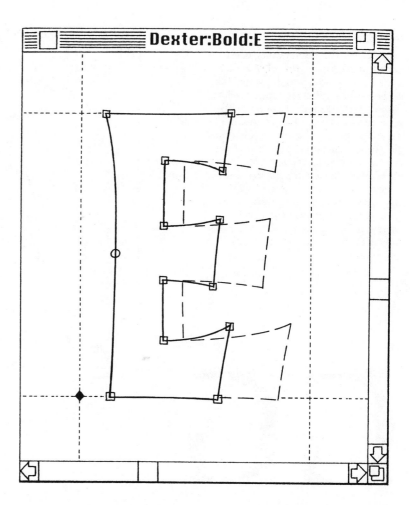

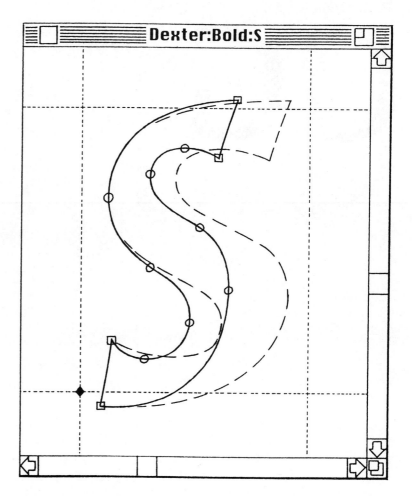

Slope

The degree of divergence from the vertical can also be set in a dialogue box, or with the slope or slanting tool. Here the designer, as always, must be prepared for nasty surprises. In this N the slope has made the upright form into an italic capital but also changed the weight relationship of the strokes: the thins becoming lighter and the diagonal becoming heavier. To correct this, the points of the inner apexes should be slightly lower (top) and higher (bottom), and inner points on the baseline and top guide line moved a little horizontally until the weight relationship is restored. Making the letter fractionally narrower will help its appearance, too. Before and after letters are shown below.

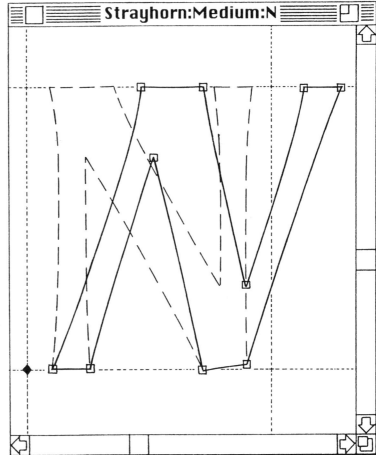

Weight

Fontographer software allows a character's weight to be changed by moving points globally in controlled increments chosen by the type designer. There are three possibilities, as illustrated here. The first, to the right of the original in the top line, has been made bolder but retains the original's height and width. The second transformation retains the original's width but has been allowed to become taller to accommodate the heavier horizontals, and in the final letter the reverse has occurred: the height has been maintained while the width has been increased. This last transformation is similar to optical scaling provided by the multiple master process. A designer could create a small-text version of a font by starting with this facility, and then making visual adjustments.

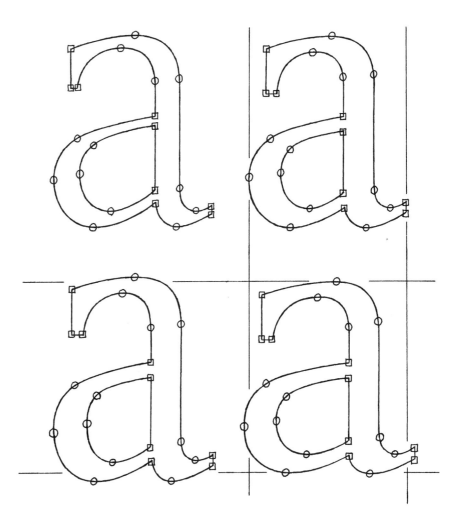

Refinements

Serifs

Serifs ending with a delightfully graceful curve may not survive the printing process unless strengthened first, one way being by terminating them in a definite cut-off, as shown in the top row at right. The slight concavity is there to stop the serif looking convex as well as adding grace to its design. Softer, rounded serifs require more points to control their curves. When working on these miniature forms the designer is grateful for the magnifying tool.

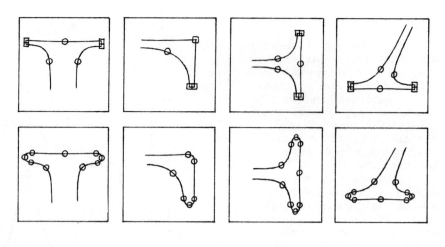

Lowercase letters have their distinctive serifs and stroke endings. Several are shown here, made with sympathy for their analogue origins but translated into digital forms that will reproduce their characteristics faithfully. For more on serifs see pages 78, 79, 86 and 87.

Script letters, faithful to their calligraphic origins, need careful placement of points and immaculate fine-tuning to maintain their cursive qualities.

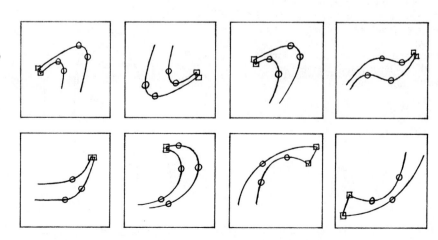

Junctions

In the photo-typesetting era, designers learned to open up junctions to allow for their tendency to fill in, and much earlier, punchcutters coped with the problem of ink squash during letter-press printing in the similar ways. Today, with lithographic printing, ink squash is not often a problem, nor is light falling unevenly on film emulsions, but junctions still need careful attention if an over-heavy appearance is to be avoided. Add an extra corner point in these tight places to let a little more air in, especially in apexes, but also where two bowls meet in certain letters. Some scripts have very steep, narrow junctions that also benefit from that extra point. Examples of all these are shown top right. It may be that the large low-resolution screen image suggests that these improvements have been overdone, but the final test is how each letter performs in print.

Every junction requires careful attention: type designers learn to place anchor points to achieve visual quality and good technical performance. Several examples are shown here.

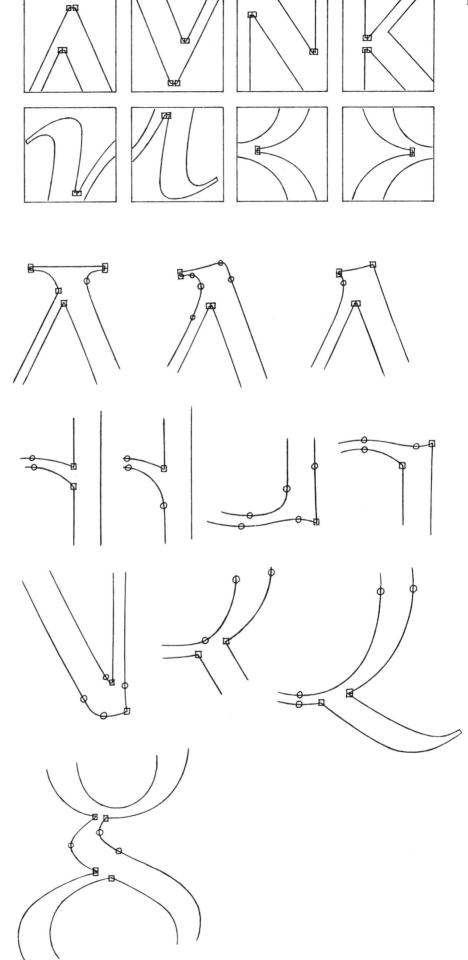

The designer who draws letters for reproduction or for type manufacture is used to paying critical attention to the minute details that automatic technical processes may affect, adding extra weight here, giving more space there. Because the digital letter can deliver such precise renderings of any letter style, especially in test prints at large sizes, it is easy to overlook the continuing need to refine serifs and junctions, in particular if the design is to work in practice.

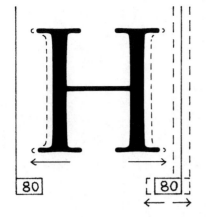

Letterfit and kerning

Letterfitting features (often called 'kerning') vary, but essentially they allow the designer to adjust the white space around each character and set simple text to test a design's performance in a limited way.

mouse to find optimum spacing. The left sidebearing is fixed but the letter can be moved sideways to alter its value, and the righthand vertical marker is moved to fix its value. Readouts give the number of units in each case; in the symmetrical letter H, left, these are of equal value.

Keywords and basic letterfit

It is common to work on a keyword that includes characters from the main letter groups. Getting these letters right first makes the design of the others easier. Typical keywords are HAMBURGEFONTS and VERBSGOHUMAN.

Each keyword letter should have a provisional width with some space on either side. Letters can now be typed in and their position moved with the

In the group below it can be seen that similar forms have similar sidebearings, all left and right verticals following the H for instance. The letter O, also symmetrical, is the next to fit, then V and so on. Letters with irregular shapes will be more difficult to get right, but eventually a viable but still provisional set of sidebearings will have been established.

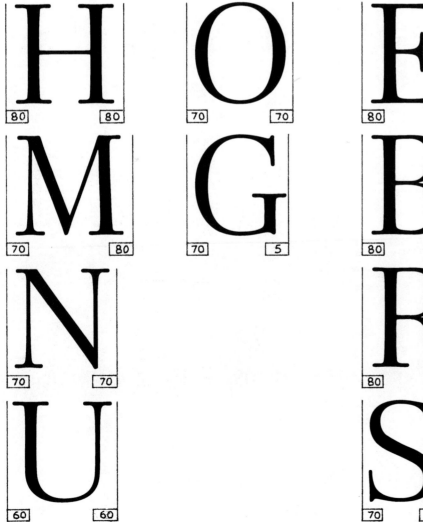

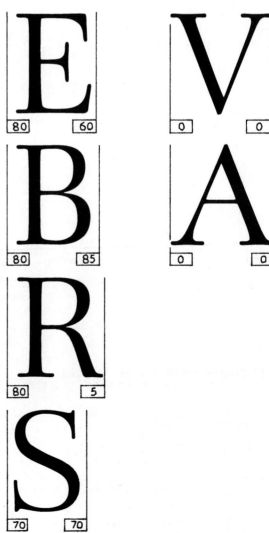

HAHBHEHGHHHMHNH
HOHRHSHUHVH
OAOBOEOGOHOMONOOO
OROSOUOVO

nanbnengnhnmnnnonrnsnunvn
oaoboeogohomonooorosouovo

Control chains

Experienced designers use H and O as control letters, setting other characters between them in a long chain. These provide essential information from which tiny changes in letterfit can be made to improve the design's overall appearance. This stage may be followed by setting up nonsense text that uses all the letters from the keyword: the piece below was composed by Fred Brady of Adobe Systems. The invisible word space value will have to be established as well to complete this test. Printouts at various sizes will also provide essential feed back.

Kerning pairs

Inevitably some pairs of characters will not combine successfully. Pairs with overhanging elements create too great a space between them, but 'kerning pairs' can be designed. The Va combination shown below is an example of the problem. With each letter confined to within its sidebearings the space between is too great, but on a shared body the characters can be given optimum spacing. During typesetting such combinations are called up where the text requires.

Oases are gorgeous
as green heaven
gush Amorous
maneuvers govern
our nature Noses
never use sorghum
as sausage sugar
Engrave some verse
on a shoehorns ear
Rough hens see a
raven move

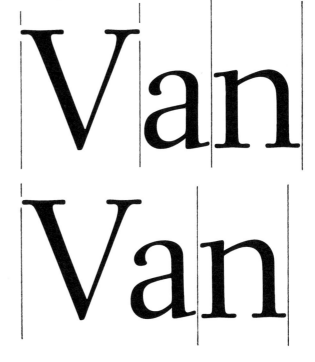

A well-fitted typeface stands a greater chance of achieving beauty and legibility: the white space is as important to design well as the black letter shapes.

Testing in a layout program

Another, more sophisticated way to test a design is to generate a working font and use it in one of the desktop publishing layout programs such as QuarkXPress or Adobe Pagemaker. Here sizes, weights and styles can be mixed and different layouts experimented with. Using the typeface in real-life layouts will help identify problems with every aspect of the design.

In the example at right the bold and light weights of a design are seen reversed out of a black ground, while below a freely-arranged lowercase text incorporates hand-drawn lettering.

Lettering is a part of everyday life, the key element of communication. It is scrawled in ballpoint, typed on keyboards and assails us in the street and in the media. To many, the letters of our alphabet are so common, so unremarkable, that they are almost invisible, so it may seem surprising that the Crafts Council should create a permanent collection of these unconsidered artifacts

In this example, simple line work encloses a bold initial that has been skewed to an angle using a software option. The vertically-set words either side are in a contrasting typeface.

IV

TO SECURE
FOR THE
WORKERS
BY HAND OR
BY BRAIN
THE FULL
FRUITS
OF THEIR
INDUSTRY
AND THE
MOST
EQUITABLE
DISTRIBUTION
THEREOF
THAT MAY
BE POSSIBLE
UPON THE
BASIS OF
COMMON
OWNERSHIP
OF THE
MEANS OF
PRODUCTION
DISTRIBUTION
AND
EXCHANGE

ACCOMMODATION IN
Bristol City
& CLIFTON VILLAGE

CHARLES
MINGUS
BLUES &
ROOTS

Layouts can be centred or arranged asymmetrically. In the top illustration a left-ranging design contrasts small light sanserif capitals with a line mixing roman and italic letters, while at left a centred design contrasts bold roman numerals screened 50% with lighter text centred beneath. In this setting the word spacing has been reduced to improve the texture in this narrow arrangement. Above, the CD cover titling uses light and bold versions of a design in a staggered layout, and below a device taken from a rubber stamp is set between lines of type in a bookplate that range left and right.

EX LIBRIS

JOHN
RYDER

Special effects

Although the computer can enhance letters by generating special effects at the touch of a key, the designer may want to create these from scratch.

Creating outline letters

The single path that defines a solid letter cannot be used as an outline itself, but can be copied, and reduced or enlarged slightly to fit inside or around the original path. Some tweaking will be necessary but a true outline letter is soon created. The amount of reduction or enlargement of the copied path determines the thickness of the outline.

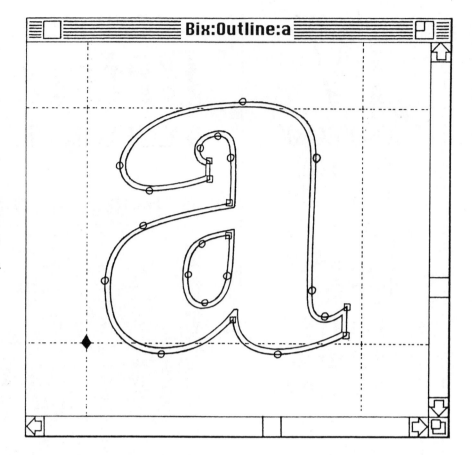

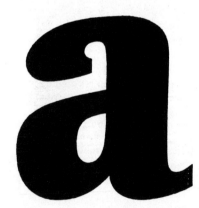
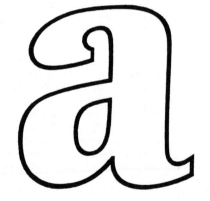
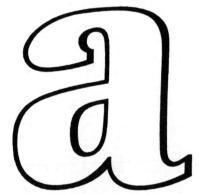

Shadow letters

Having made an outline character by the process described above, points can be shifted laterally and vertically to offset the outer path to create an outline of varying thickness yielding a shadow effect, as in the last three examples shown here.

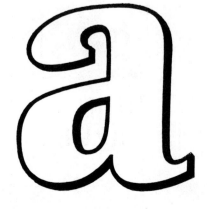
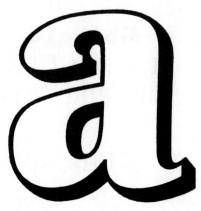

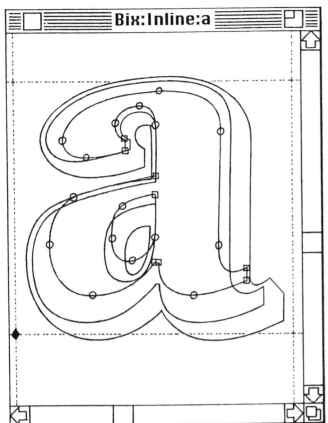
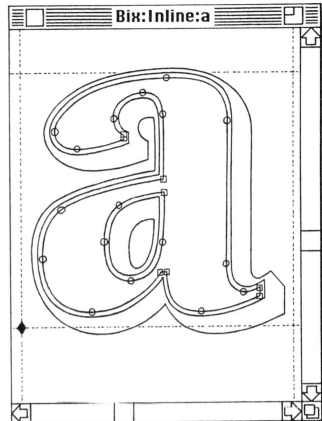

Filled outline letters

A reduced copy of the original letter is shown above, pasted into the character window of the shadow letter described on the previous page. When the points are manipulated so that the two letters are separated by a continuous and even line, a positive form with a white in-line and shadow has been created. Two versions are shown right, one with the solid centre shaded to give another graphic effect. Two-colour printing or tints could be used to exploit such letters.

Drop shadow effects

Computer-generated shadow effects rarely work, especially when, as here, the letter is relatively light. Far better to avoid such obviously corny tricks of the computer and design your own special effects.

Computer-aided graphic design: a multi-layered title

The creation of complex logotypes or titles would at one time take many hours of drawing on overlays to separate the various elements, but now, thanks to software programs such as Illustrator and Freehand, this is a less time-consuming process. This example of computer-aided design starts with a sketch, right. After scanning, each word is digitized separately, either with the pen tool, or using the auto-trace option and editing out the unwanted points in the outline path.

First layer

The word Art is a script-based letter (see pages 38 and 39) with a swash initial, so the digital conversion needs to be faithful to that tradition of ebullient written forms which are conveyed in the drawn sketch.

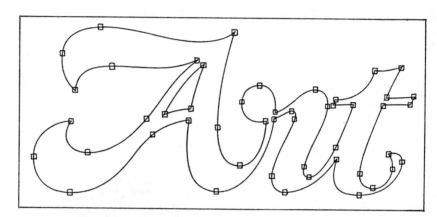

Second layer

Like the first word, this ampersand should have a fluid cursive character.

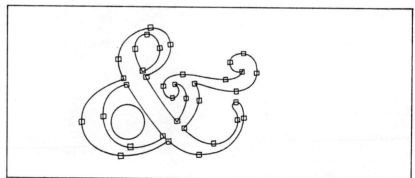

Third layer

By contrast, this word is in a plain sanserif style. Note the smallness of the dot that has to fit inside the counter of the ampersand.

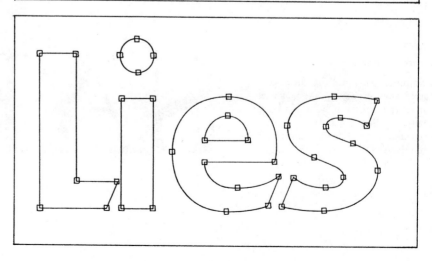

Background layer

The ground on which the design fits makes a fourth layer, each digital outline pasted in place and a reversed image created with a software option. Four layers have been made more accurately and speedily than by traditional drawing methods.

Further options

The designer can enhance the letters and background using special effects provided by separate plug-in filters, some of which are indicated here. But these simulated textures and airbrush effects may gild the lily and should be used with restraint.

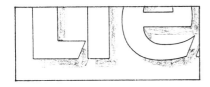

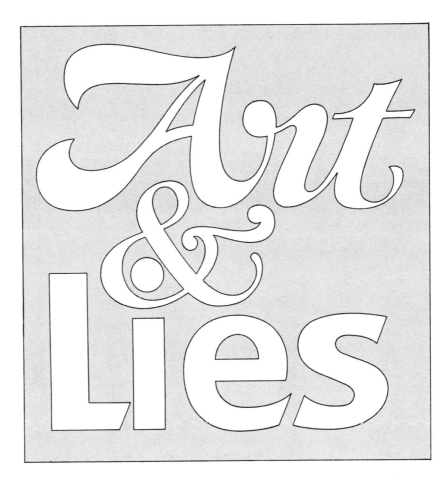

Final version

Such a title lends itself to an expressive treatment, but, as when creating a design using conventional equipment – pens, brushes, inks – the designer has to decide how far to go. The last thing that's wanted is a design that proclaims its computer origins. Computer art is, of course, something else and outside the scope of this book.

On pages 114 to 119 the evolution of a
typeface is described. When this design
went into production the drawings (all
1000 of them) were digitized by Monotype and the typeface, named Ellington,
was released in four weights in 1990.
Later, the company decided to commission a sanserif version, to be created
digitally from the Ellington design,
without any preliminary drawing. The
new typeface is called Strayhorn and its
creation is outlined here.

A digital conversion

After importing into Fontographer, the
first task was to edit out the serifs in the
light and extra bold fonts, leaving
slightly swelled stems, and to make all
the light strokes slightly heavier to
achieve balanced characters. Many subtle changes proved necessary as the new
design slowly assumed its own character.

Shorn of their serifs, the capitals
looked too tall, and so were reduced in
height by 5%. Serifs add a lot of interest

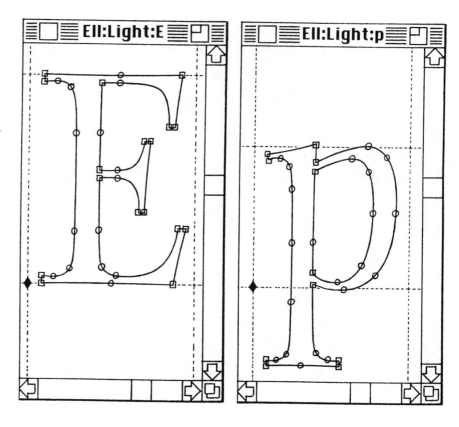

ELLINGTON

Light/Medium

Bold/Extra Bold

Light/Medium

Bold/Extra Bold

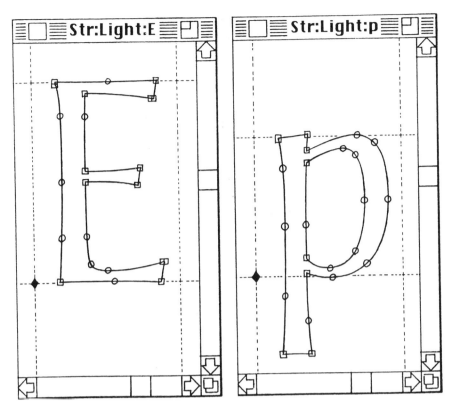

to letterforms and their removal left these letters looking naked, with their shortcomings exposed. If anything the simplicity of sanserif makes this a harder letter to get right compared to the apparently more complex roman seriffed forms, and so it proved in this case. With its lively cursive forms and generous serifs, the italic lowercase of Ellington was particularly difficult to adapt.

Retaining some of the life in the capitals was a problem too, but this was helped by making the spread at the top left of the verticals more definite by adding an extra point. With another on the upswept termination of the lower horizontal of E, the extra points were enough to give an almost calligraphic swing through the letter. This is reminiscent of the 'east-bound serif' described on page 82, and such points were added where appropriate to the other characters in the fonts. With such devices even the plainest letters can be made to live.

When the light and extra bold fonts had been converted, Fontographer's powerful interpolation software generated the intermediate weights.

STRAYHORN

Light/**Medium**

Bold/Extra Bold

Light/Medium

Bold/Extra Bold

An uncial-based design

Inspiration for a typeface can come from many sources, ancient and modern. The idea for this design came from the group of eighth-century letters shown right. Their almost art deco appearance was exciting and seemed to be a visual equivalent of the piano-playing of Count Basie.

With such little material to go on, the rest of the alphabet was drawn from

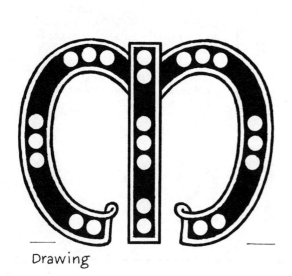

Drawing

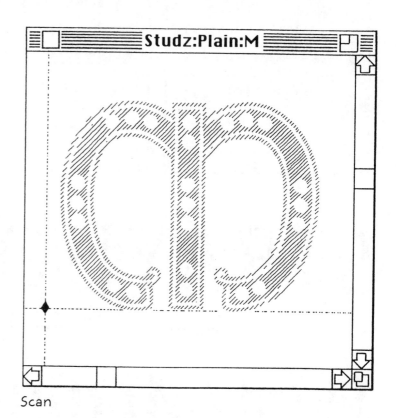

Scan

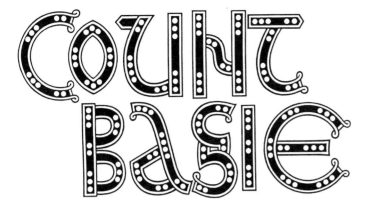

contemporary uncial sources (see page 26) or invented, as were W, X and Y, to suit the general style. With many parallel paths to control, digitizing this design was an exacting process. The circles inside the strokes were conveniently drawn with the software's circle drawing tool. Naming a typeface is often the most difficult part, but in this case was easy. It just had to be called *Studz*.

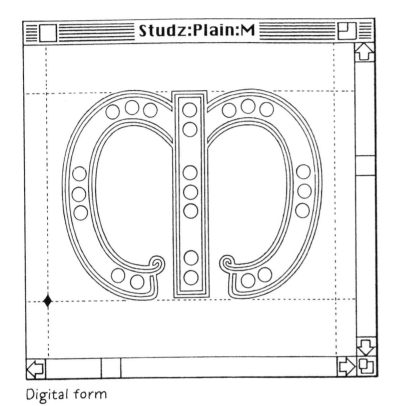

Digital form

Print

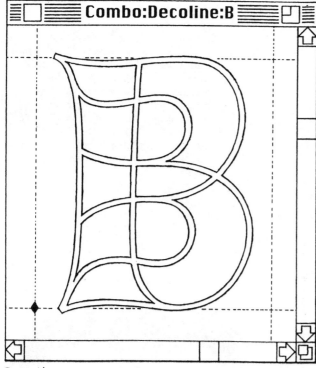

Decoline

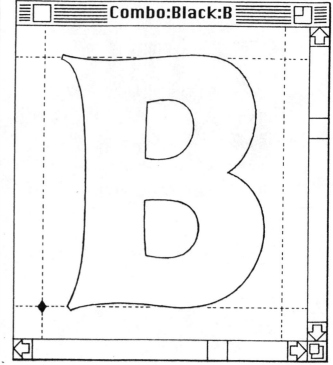

Black

A display family

Letters in a medieval manuscript book, whose forms were embellished with fluid lines and colour, inspired this design. Such a letter, with its twisting, curvy inner spaces, would allow users to fill these with colour or texture by hand, or by turning the letters into outlines in Illustrator. It would be a truly interactive typeface.

The version called *Decoline* was digitized first, then all the inner paths were

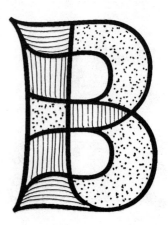

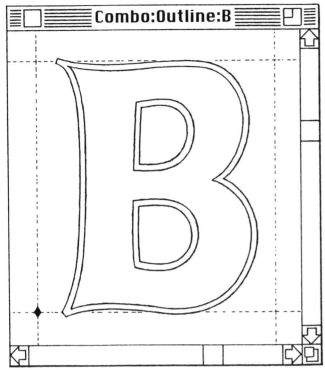

Outline

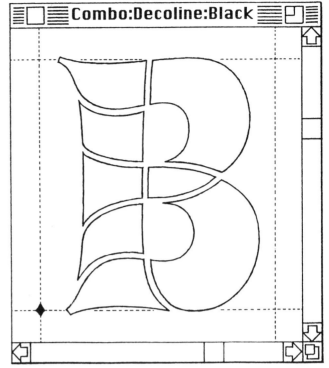

Decoline black

edited out to make a plain version, *Black*. Next, the crossover paths were removed from *Decoline* to make an open version, *Outline*. Finally, *Decoline Black* was developed, a design that reversed the effect of the original version. Laser prints of the keyword showed the decorative potential of these letters.

Once in digital form, the development of variations was simple, and seeing the first version on screen sparked the ideas for these variations.

Carving letters in stone and wood

Stone carving: tools, materials and techniques

Carving letters in stone or slate requires only a few tools; chisels of varying widths, a dummy, sharpening stones and an easel or banker to support the work. It is usual to carve letters with the stone upright and this is the method described here, although some carvers prefer to work with the stone in a horizontal position. Apart from the specialised tools described below the carver will need only a square and straight edge to help lay out the inscription, and water to wash off the dust and pencil marks when it is finished.

Chisels Modern tungsten-tipped chisels have the great advantage over all-steel tools that they retain a sharp cutting edge for much longer. A steel chisel, finely tapered to a slim edge, will cut a precise line in slate that possibly the tungsten-tipped tool cannot match, but good, well-tempered steel chisels are virtually impossible to obtain today. Tungsten-tipped chisels are classified for cutting marble or granite, blue for marble, red for granite. Marble chisels are suitable for all kinds of slate and stone. Four sizes will be sufficient for most work, $\frac{1}{4}''$, $\frac{3}{8}''$,

$\frac{1}{2}''$, with a 1″ chisel for removing waste stone from large letters. Claw tools and points are useful for carving backgrounds.

Dummy A round mallet made of either a mixture of lead and zinc, or iron, weighing about 1½ lb. The iron type is excellent and long-lasting, and while the lead and zinc type give a slightly softer blow that some carvers prefer, repeated use can deform or even break them.

Hammer For heavier work use a steel hammer weighing about 1¾ lb, the handle of which needs to be a short manageable length.

Sharpening stones Green grit stones made in several grades are used for rubbing the tungsten tip to a sharp edge. Stones are best kept immersed in water and used wet. Circular stones on power grinders need to be used with great care because the high speed can easily cause the removal of too much precious tungsten. Only grind worn chisels to restore cutting angles, then use a fine grit stone to achieve a sharp edge by gentle rubbing, first one side

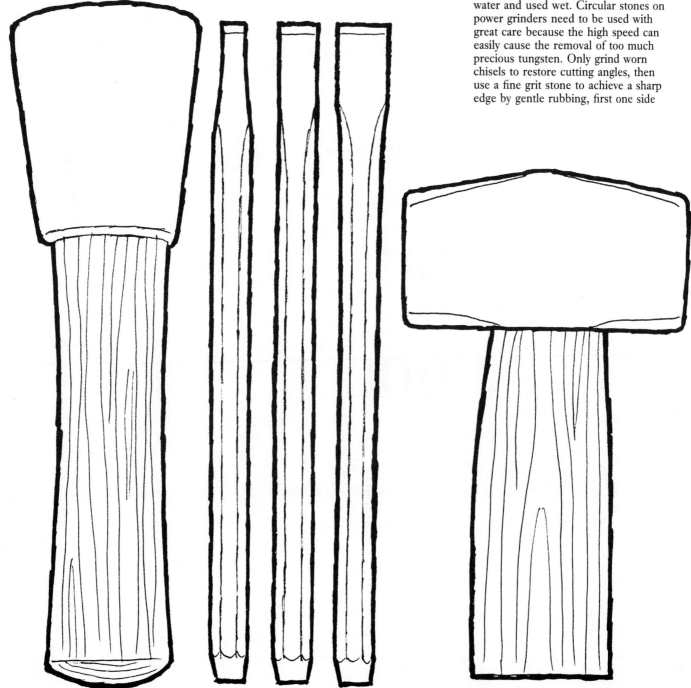

then the other. Tools that lose their squareness and become oblique or rounded should be held edge on to the grinding wheel and the edge gently squared up, followed by grinding and rubbing to recover sharpness.

Silicon carbide paper Abrasive paper available in several grades, used wet to rub stone or slate to improve the surface or to remove pencil lines and paint. Use the finer grades on slate and rub with a circular motion.

Pencils Use hard pencils (9H) to rule guide lines and slightly softer (2H) for drawing letters. Lead pencil does not show up well on slate so a white crayon pencil may be used for drawing lines and letters.

Easel The drawing here shows a substantial adjustable easel that will support stones and slates safely. Used with chairs of various heights the adjustable support allows the carver to work comfortably. For tall pieces he may need to stand on a box, and when cutting the lowest line on a gravestone that rests on the floor he will be forced into a squatting position. The professional carver needs to retain a youthful flexibility!

Lighting The best lighting is overhead, with supplementary side lighting that can be adjusted to suit the work in progress. A single light bulb hanging on a long flex will do, but a lamp on a stand is better.

Materials The limestones from Portland and Purbeck in Dorset are excellent for inscription carving, the harder Purbeck stones, being full of shells, can be polished to give a rich brown/grey colour that provides a contrast with carved letters. Stones from other parts of England that are good for carving include Ancaster, Forest of Dean and Eric Gill's favourite Hopton Wood, and the imported marble called Nabrasina is a good stone with a hard even texture.

Slate is a very attractive material for lettering. The light incised line stands out against the darker background making slate a good material for inscriptions indoors. In outdoor use weathering greatly reduces this contrast. Grey Welsh slate and the harder green slates from Cumbria, some with attractive markings, are good for inscriptions.

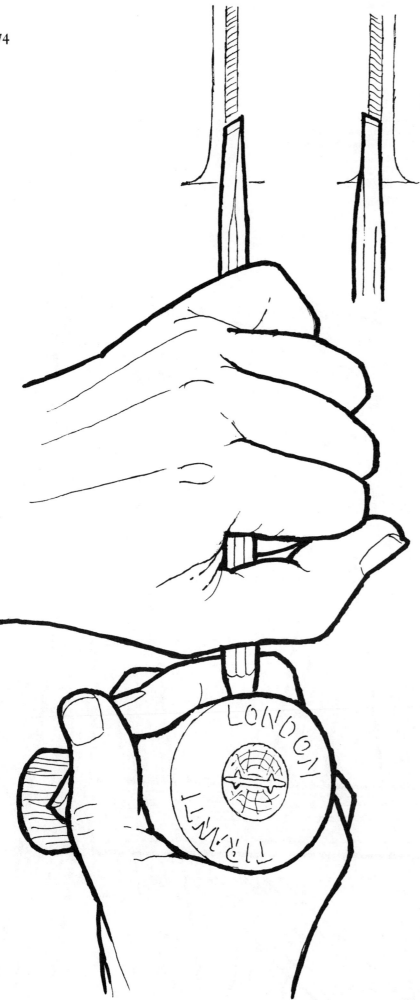

Carving techniques

The drawings on this and the following four pages show hands in several carving positions. In the cutting of a vee-section letter—the simplest and quickest way to make a letter in stone—two angles are critical; the angle of the chisel to the stone's surface, which has to be not so steep that the chisel digs in nor so shallow that it skids across the surface, and the angle the cutting edge makes with the stone. This angle should be about 45° so that as the chisel cuts first one side then the other a vee-cut of approximately 90° will be made. These angles are shown in the illustrations below.

With the chisel held lightly the dummy is used to drive it gently into the stone using wrist movements only. With practice the interaction of chisel, dummy and stone produces a sure touch in the carver; he will sense when he is cutting too deeply and become aware of changes in the note of regular tapping that may indicate trouble.

When carving a vertical stroke the dummy can be held as shown on this page, with the hand directly behind the chisel, or as shown right with the hand to the side to give finer control.

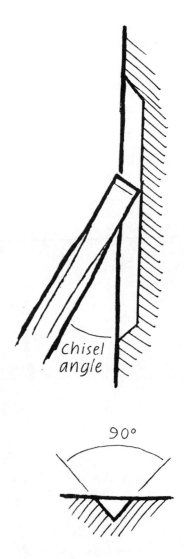

chisel angle

90°

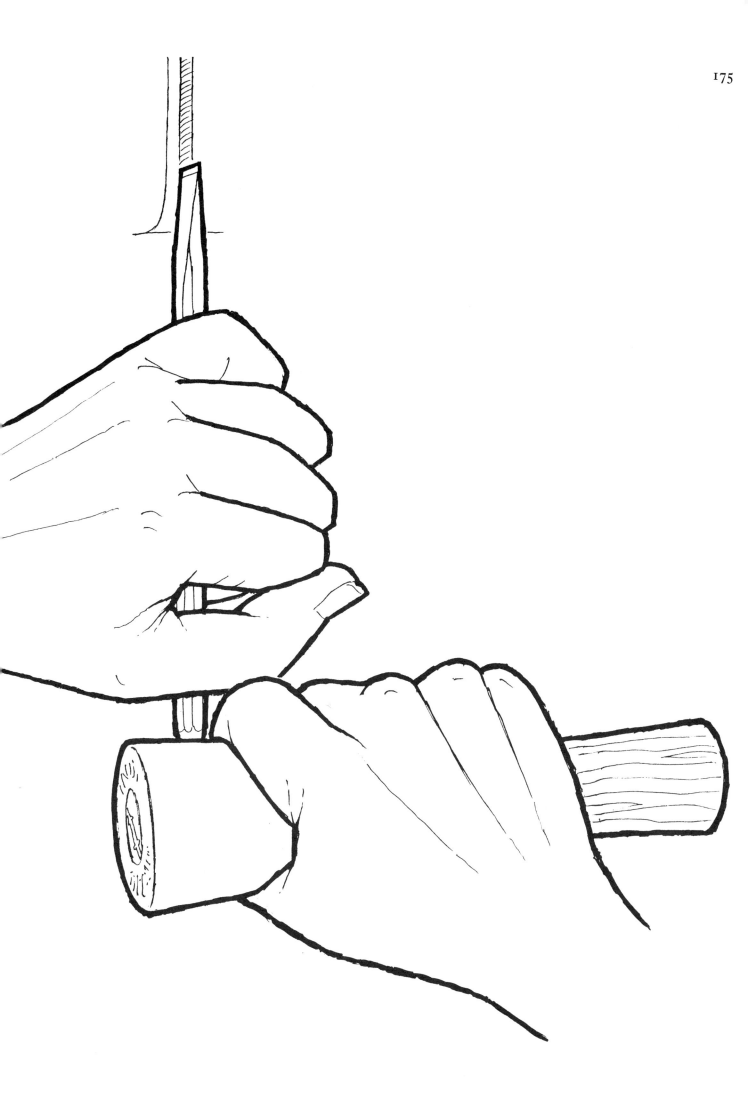

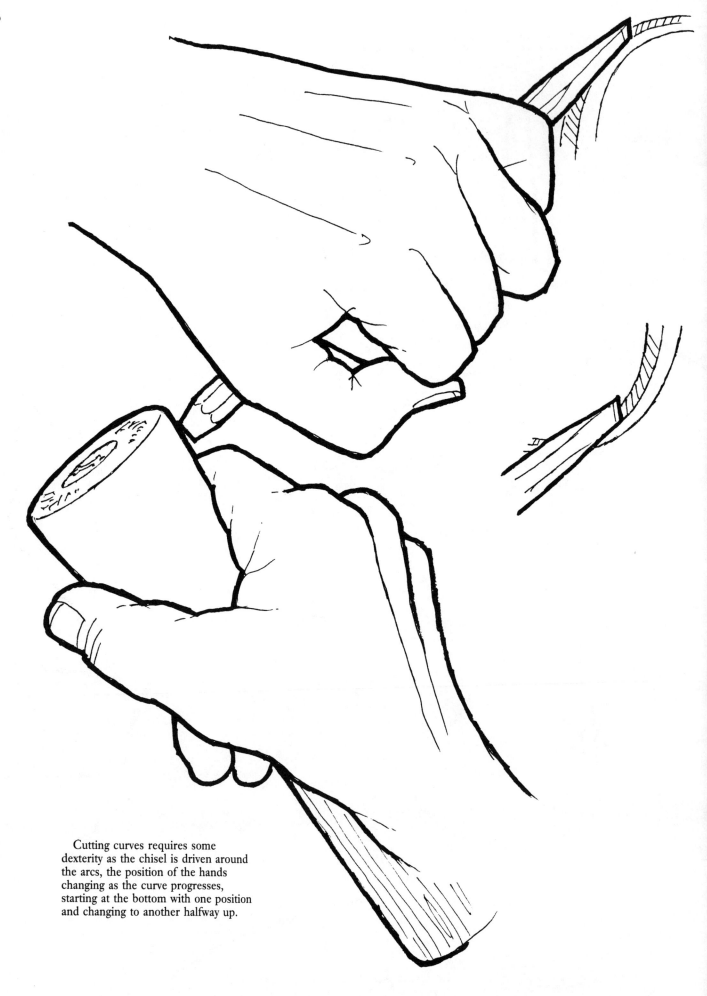

Cutting curves requires some dexterity as the chisel is driven around the arcs, the position of the hands changing as the curve progresses, starting at the bottom with one position and changing to another halfway up.

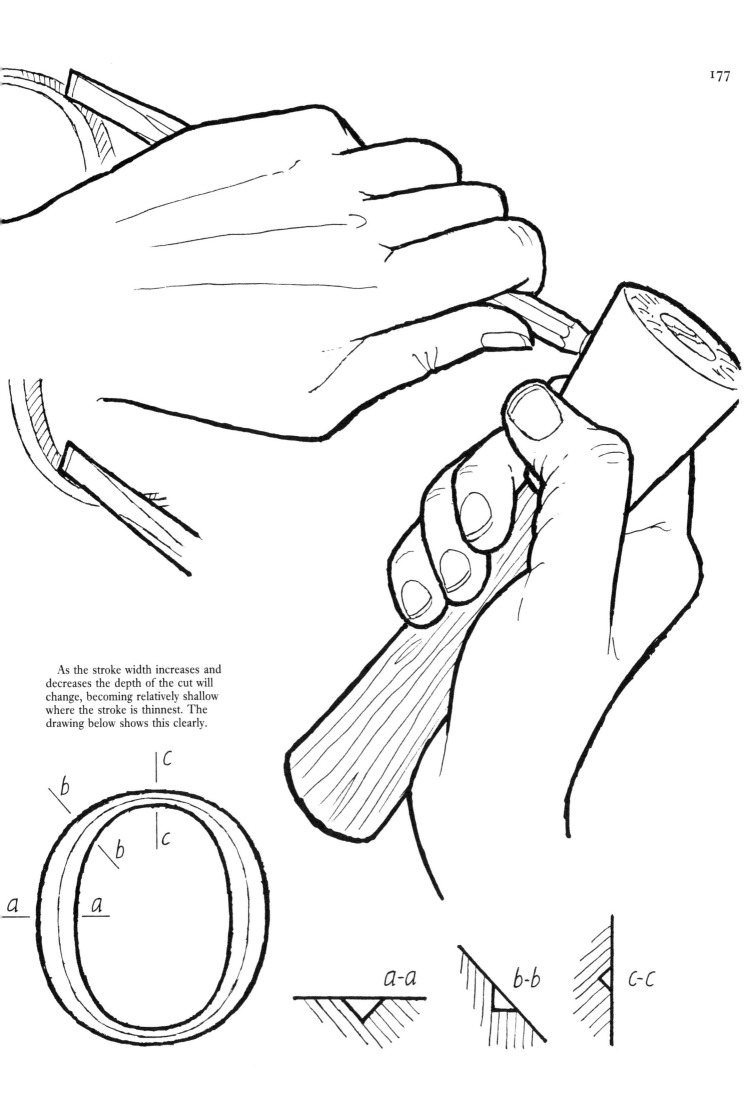

As the stroke width increases and decreases the depth of the cut will change, becoming relatively shallow where the stroke is thinnest. The drawing below shows this clearly.

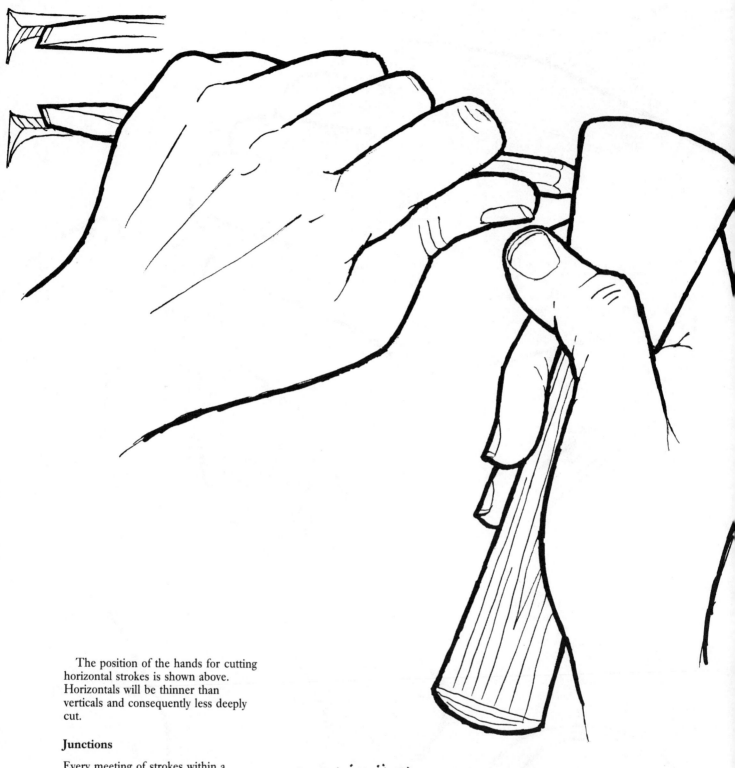

The position of the hands for cutting horizontal strokes is shown above. Horizontals will be thinner than verticals and consequently less deeply cut.

Junctions

Every meeting of strokes within a letter is a hazard in stone carving. To minimise the danger of stone breaking away where horizontals cut across verticals from the right, steepen the chisel angle as the chisel approaches the junction so that the cutting edge is directed into the stone. Alternatively cut the horizontals first; the deeper vertical cut is less likely to break the stone as the chisel cuts across the shallower horizontal. Take special care at apexes, particularly in B and M, if possible cutting away from them. One advantage of working flat is that this is more easily done. Sometimes it is easier to lay down the dummy and push the chisel with both hands in these delicate situations.

Avoid unnecessary trouble with
K by allowing the strokes barely to
touch instead of merging.

Serifs

Originating largely from brush writing,
serifs have been part of the inscriptional letter almost from the earliest
times. Their treatment may be quite
varied, as shown right, finely drawn
out, bold and type-like or minimal but
elegantly shaped. Serifs should always
blend smoothly with the stroke.

Stone and slate

Lettering in stone needs to be carved
strongly enough to produce the
shadows that are an essential aid to
legibility, but lettering in slate can be
very finely carved because the fine-
grained material and strong contrast
between the letter and the background
encourage this. Oiling will darken the
slate and increase this contrast.

Limestone is the best material for
the novice letter carver. Slate is easy
to carve but its fine texture shows up
every imperfection in cutting, making
it a frustrating material for the
inexperienced carver.

Carving styles

With a sharp chisel and fine materials
almost any letterform, even complex
scripts, can be carved. The top line
shows the typical serifs and junctions
of italic writing translated into a stone-
carved form. Below is shown a modified, more easily carved, adaptation
which produces a more angular, less
flowing, perhaps more inscriptional
form. The tight curves in scripts take
some skill in carving, the chisel making
a series of very short, scraping cuts as
it is driven around the curve, and the
carver may wish to avoid very angular
scripts for this reason. Choice of style
will depend also on the material being
worked.

Correcting mistakes

Scratches caused by chisel slips may
be rubbed away by the gentle use of
silicon carbide paper. More serious
errors can be made good with a
mixture of stone dust and an epoxy
resin such as Araldite. Once set hard
this can be rubbed down and carved so
as to be undetectable—except to the
carver.

Carving sequence

The stages in carving a capital R in limestone are shown here. Guidelines are drawn with a very hard pencil (9H) and a less hard pencil (2H) is used to sketch in the letter (1). Using a chisel slightly wider than the vertical stroke the first cuts are made on the right of the vertical and the tail leaving an uneven left edge (2). Subsequent cuts on the left even up this edge and establish the vee-section that now serves as a guide for further carving (3). The serifs are completed and carving continues until both strokes are smoothly finished. The horizontal is carved and the inside of the curved bowl begun—it is good practice to carve the inside curves of enclosed spaces first (4). The outer curve is cut leading into the top serif (5). When the letter is judged to be satisfactory all remaining pencil lines can be erased (6). Remember that the pencilled letter is only a guide and the final letter must be judged as a three-dimensional form defined by light and shadow.

A rather different technique for carving letters in slate is shown below. The letter is first painted in white gouache (1), then roughed in with a chisel and the paint washed off (2). The carving is now completed entirely by eye (3). If the slate is to be oiled this should be done after (2) and left for several days before the final carving is done. For more information on oiling slate see page 183.

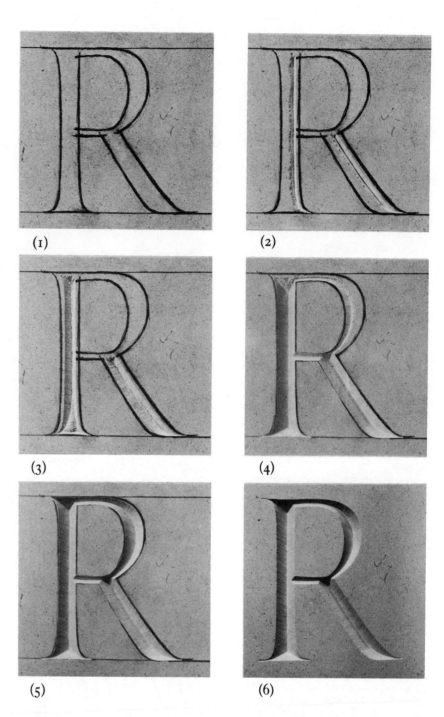

(1) (2) (3) (4) (5) (6)

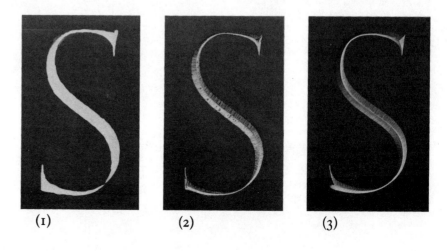

(1) (2) (3)

Carving large letters

The larger the letter the more like
sculpture it becomes, so keep one
chisel of the correct width for the final
carving and use a wider chisel and a
hammer to cut directly down into the
stone to remove waste material quickly,
cutting one side then the other and
keeping well away from the letter's
edge. Do this on the curves too, but
use a narrower chisel.

The final carving will go beyond
the rough edges of this preliminary
excavation and the chisel retained for
this purpose will remain sharp for
several letters. In the letter above the
serifs are suitably strong and blunt
while blending elegantly with the letter
strokes.

Rubbings

It is a good idea to take rubbings to
check an inscription's progress because
undetected wobbles and variations in
stroke weight may show up later in
other lighting conditions. This is
particularly important if the letters are
to be painted and the soft effects of
light and shade replaced by the hard
edge of painted colour. Use detail
paper and heel-ball, obtainable from
shoe repairers. A final rubbing may
be made as a record, although a
photograph is more useful, especially
for exhibiting and showing to clients.
Virtually all the photography for this
book was done with a 35mm SLR
camera.

(1)

(2)

(3)

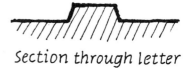

Section through letter

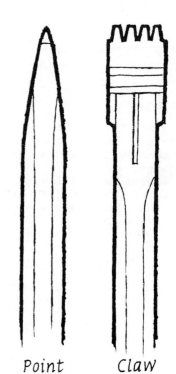

Point   Claw

Letters suitable for relief carving

Relief carving

Much more work is involved in carving letters in relief, but the stronger forms will show up better than incised letters in poor light and have a distinctive, sculptural impact.

In the illustration shown left the bold letters are drawn with little contrast in the strokes and the chiselled line is clear of the pencilled edge (1). Using a hammer and various chisels the background is lowered to the desired depth, which need not be deep to obtain a strong effect, and the letters stand out clearly (2). After the letters' final edges have been carved the roughly carved background may be further worked to produce a smooth surface or a texture from a claw tool or a point (3). The heavier work necessary to carve backgrounds is best done with the stone in a horizontal position. Remember to protect the stone by laying it on a soft material.

(1)

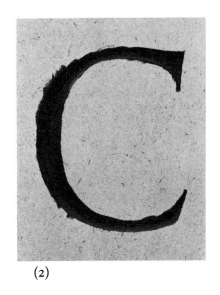

(2)

(3)

Painting and gilding

Inscriptions in stone may be coloured to improve legibility or for decorative effect. The stages in painting a letter are shown above, starting with the unpainted letter (1) which should be given a coat of a clear sealer before the paint is applied (2). There is no need to be painstaking about painting only the incised letter; it is easier to apply the paint freely and remove any excess by rubbing the surface with silicon carbide paper, leaving a clearly painted letter (3).

For indoor work use a paint that dries matt and waterproof. Plaka is excellent and is available in a variety of colours. This paint can be used outdoors, too, but gloss paints will last longest, although their shine can seem unsympathetic.

An alternative to paint is gold leaf, which has a quite stunning effect on slate. The stages in gilding are shown below, starting with the cut letter (4) which should be sealed with red or yellow ochre oil paint mixed with gold size. When this is dry a coat of a 12- or 24-hour gold size mixed with cadmium yellow oil paint is applied and when almost dry loose gold leaf, cut into manageable strips, is picked up with a flat soft brush that has been brushed against the hair to produce static electricity, and gently laid in the letter. Press the leaf home with a pointed brush so that every part of the letter is covered in gold, brushing out surplus fragments (5). After several days rub down the surface with fine silicon carbide paper and water until the finished letter stands out sharply. A final enrichment is achieved if the slate

is now oiled with a 50–50 mixture of linseed oil and turpentine (6).

The final rubbing down of stone and slate should be done with running water playing over the surface, so that any slurry is washed away and does not remain to dull the letters.

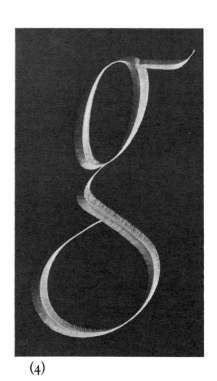

(4)

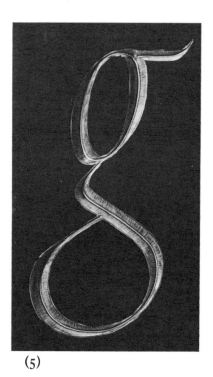

(5)

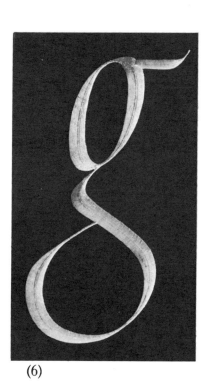

(6)

The principal differences between stone and wood as they affect the carver are the fibrous nature of the wood and the grain which requires constant vigilance if splits are to be avoided, and the necessity to work from several directions to remove surplus wood from a letter, unlike stone which obligingly crumbles and falls away under the chisel's impact. For these reasons wood carving requires several tools, especially gouges of various curves, as illustrated below. With tools from the following list the carver will be well equipped, although

he may discover supplementary carving tools to help working letters in relief.

Chisels Straight carving chisels in sizes $\frac{1}{8}''$, $\frac{1}{4}''$, $\frac{3}{8}''$ and $\frac{1}{2}''$, with a wide chisel for cutting down into stroke centres and a skew chisel for getting in deep to remove obstinate fibres.

Gouges Several widths and curvatures will be useful, some wide and shallow, and others narrow and tightly curved for shaping curves in some letters.

Mallet Most carving is done by using both hands to push and guide the chisel or gouge, but a small mallet,

preferably of lignum vitae, a very hard and heavy wood, is essential for some carving work.

Oilstones Sharp tools are an absolute necessity for wood carving so it is essential to have an India oilstone, slipstones of different curvatures to fit the gouges and a tin of thin oil. Chisels are rubbed on both sides to obtain a sharp edge. Gouges are rubbed with a rotational motion around the outer curve, and the burr raised on the concave inner edge is gently rubbed off with a slipstone of corresponding curvature, taking care not to make a

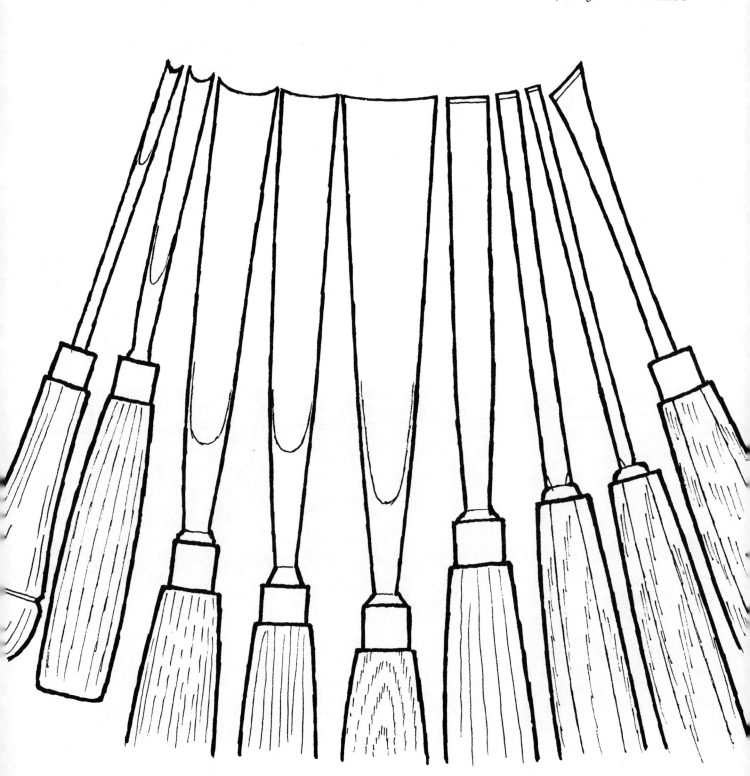

bevel on the inside. If grinding is necessary to restore a tool's edge use a handwheel and avoid overheating which will remove the temper from the steel.

Sandpaper Keep a range of grades for preparing and finishing, and always use with the grain of the wood.

Clamps It is usual to work with the wood on a bench to which it must be securely clamped. The kind of clamp illustrated here is easily adjusted and removed. Any strong table will serve as a bench.

Masking tape 2″ tape can be used to cover the area being worked on, providing a drawing surface and protection for the wood.

Pencils Use a medium pencil such as HB to avoid scoring the wood surface.

Other equipment The tools listed above are sufficient for cutting vee-section and relief letters in wood, but for carving three dimensional letters other tools such as rasps, files and saws will be necessary. Power driven bandsaws and routers, while not essential, are highly desirable and time-saving tools.

Materials There are many woods suitable for letter carving but some are not easy to obtain. Timber stores will invariably sell pine, a soft wood that is easy to carve with very sharp tools. Parana pine, a slightly harder wood, is good to carve but liable to split. Lime is another fairly soft wood that carves easily making it a good wood for beginners. Medium hard woods include sycamore, ash and maple, but, like the soft woods, are often a little bland in appearance. Hard woods such as oak, elm, mahogany and teak are richer in colour and distinctively grained. It is easier to carve letters in the more expensive hard woods which are also less prone to bruising than softer timbers.

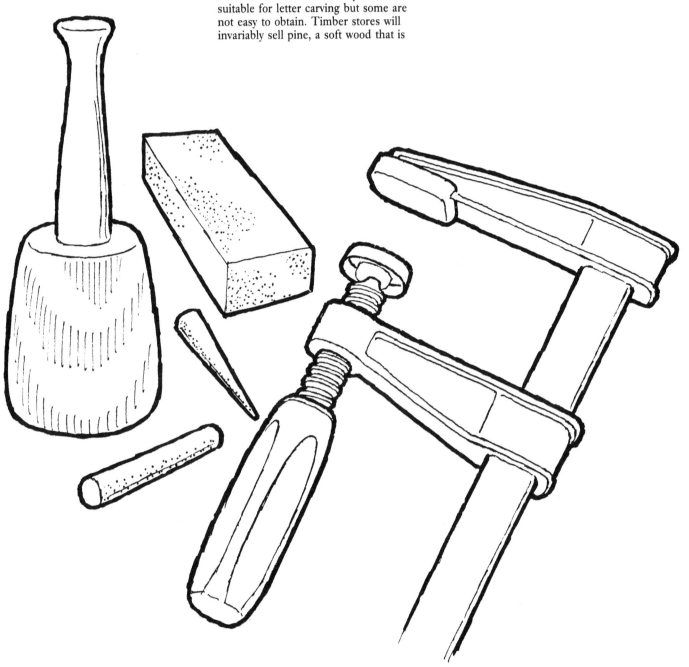

Wood Grain

The most important factor to affect letter carving in wood is the grain. Cutting across the grain, as shown left, the chisel's direction must change as the angle of approach changes, cutting from bottom to top on the outside and from top to bottom on the inside. This careful method will ensure that the chisel never digs into the grain causing a split. Apexes, such as those in A, M, N, V, W are particularly liable to break away if the grain direction is ignored. Of course, these mistakes can be glued back but it is far better not to make them in the first place.

Carving technique

The technique described here for carving vee-section letters works well with a minimum number of tools, the straights being carved with the chisels, and curves with chisels and gouges. It is possible to carve curves completely with a straight chisel if it is angled to slice through the wood, a skew chisel is better but even so great skill is required to keep the chisel from biting into the curve. An alternative method using only a vee-section parting tool is not shown because these tools are very difficult to sharpen and do not allow enough fine control in shaping letter strokes.

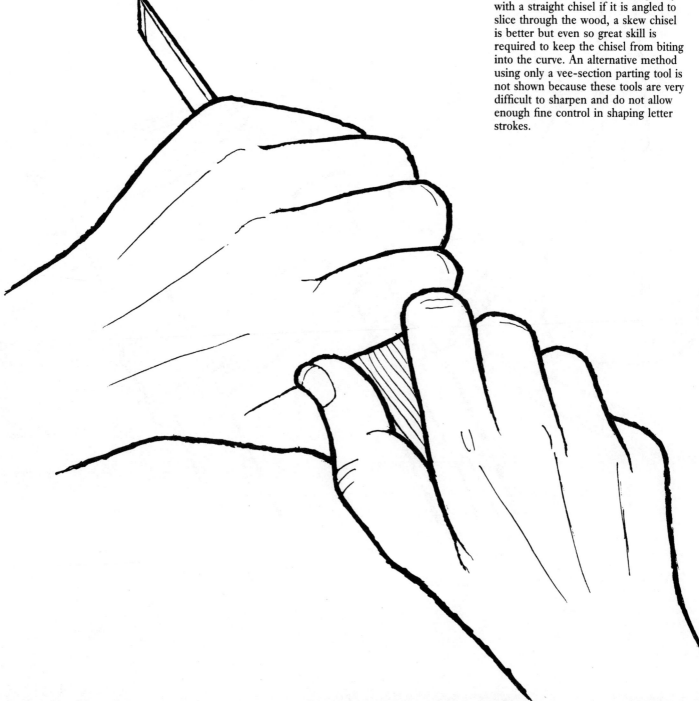

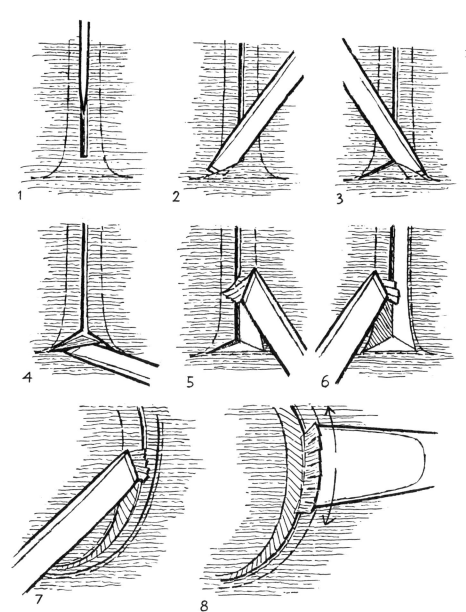

The drawings on the right show the carving sequence, beginning by using a mallet to drive a wide chisel vertically into the letter's centre line (1). Next the triangle of the serif can be removed in three cuts using the mallet and chisel (2, 3 and 4). The waste wood inside the letter is then removed in two pieces, right and left, to make the vee-cut, using a mallet or pushing the chisel by hand (5 and 6).

A similar beginning is made with curved letters, but using a narrow chisel to cut down vertically along the centre line, remembering to cut less deeply as the stroke width narrows. Then a straight chisel is used to remove the inner waste wood, taking care to cut with the grain (7). The outer waste is removed with a gouge of suitable curvature, driven down towards the centre of the vee-cut and twisted from side to side in a slicing motion (8). With the majority of the waste wood removed carving can continue, hand-pushing chisels and gouges until the vee-cut is completed. Keep a sharp narrow chisel to shape serifs and a skew chisel to clean out the bottom of the serif triangle.

Tightly curved gouges are essential for cutting the sharp curves in italic letters, as shown below.

Carving sequence

These photographs show the stages in cutting letters in wood using masking tape to protect the surface. The only disadvantage is that the grain is obscured, so do not use masking tape if the grain is particularly distinctive requiring subtle adjustments to the letterforms.

Draw guidelines and letters in pencil on the tape (1), then rough in the letters with chisels and gouges (2) as described on page 186. The final carving can proceed (3) and the tape is then removed to reveal the completed inscription (4). If the letters are to be painted this can be done easily before the masking tape is removed.

An alternative to using masking tape is to fix a drawing of the lettering to the wood surface with a spray adhesive. Whichever method is used remember that the carved letters should be studied critically after the tape or drawing is removed: there may still be room for improvement when they are defined entirely by light and shade.

(1)

(2)

(3)

(4)

TO BE CONCERNED WITH
THE SHAPES OF LETTERS
IS TO WORK IN AN ANCIENT
& FUNDAMENTAL MATERIAL

TO BE CONCERNED WITH
THE SHAPES OF LETTERS
IS TO WORK IN AN ANCIENT
& FUNDAMENTAL MATERIAL

Grain direction

An optical illusion can occur if
relatively small letters are arranged in
lines along the direction of the grain,
making the lines appear to diverge, as
in this quotation from W. A. Dwiggins.
Be aware of this possibility when
planning an inscription in wood and
consider the advantage of vertical
grain's minimal disturbance. A further
advantage of vertical grain is that the
inner apexes of letters such as this W
are in no danger of breaking away.

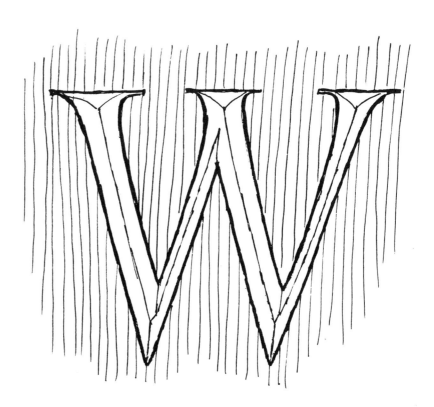

Knife carving

Carving wood with a knife is an ancient
skill that can be used most effectively
to cut letters, a technique favoured by
Will Carter whose hands are seen in
the photographs opposite. One obvious
virtue of knife carving is that so few
tools are required, and although it is
perfectly possible to work with a single
knife a gouge is helpful for cutting
curves. Will Carter uses only four
gouges, and his tool kit fits comfortably
into a cigar box.

Because the knife has to be gripped
firmly it is important that the handle is
shaped to suit the carver's hand. Two
knives are shown here, one having an
elegant handle shaped to fit the thumb
at the top with a recess above the blade
to receive the index finger of the other
hand. The handle of the other knife is
similarly shaped for thumb and finger
but is longer and simpler in profile;
a knife for cutting large letters when
considerable force must be applied.
The knife blade is sharpened with the
honed edge on the left. This makes the
knife tend to move towards the centre
of the letter lessening the danger of
over-cutting.

The main technical difference
between knife carving and chiselling
is that the knife is generally pulled
towards the carver with a slicing effect.
To make a cut the knife is gripped in
the right hand—a left-handed carver
will use a knife with its handle shaped
the opposite way to those shown here
and with the blade honed to the right.
The knife is held almost vertically to
the letter stroke that is to be cut, and

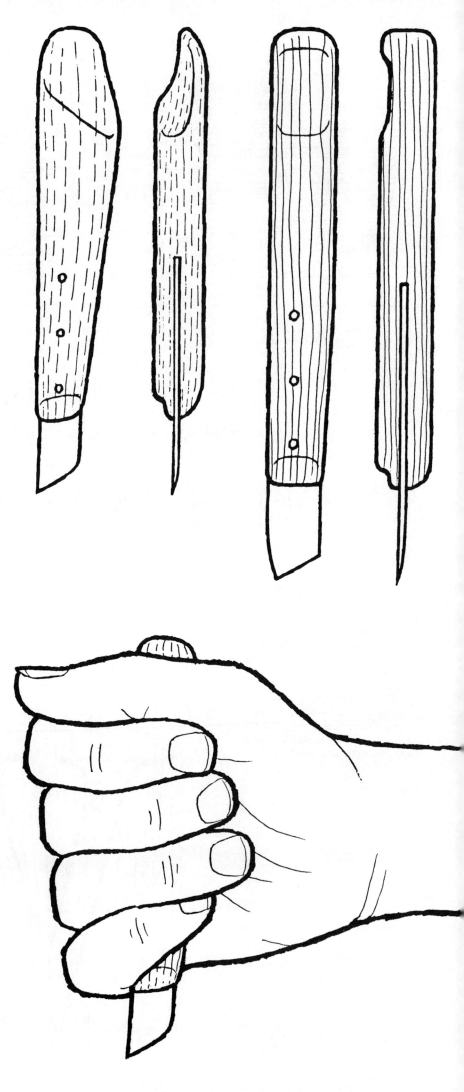

angled to the right to make one side of the vee-sectioned incision. Control is obtained by the pressure of the index finger of the other hand against the knife's handle as it is pulled back cutting into the wood. The carver's eye view shown in the drawing illustrates this clearly. To make the opposite side of the vee-cut it is necessary to turn the work around so that the letter is upside down. Working from side to side the cut will deepen as the width of the cut increases until the stroke is completed. As the photograph (below left) shows, the knife may be held differently as it cuts deeply into serifs or refines a detail. With practice the carver is able to manipulate the knife in many ways apart from the main method described here, pushing as well as pulling it to shape the letters he is cutting. As always when working in wood it is essential to observe carefully the grain direction to prevent the knife being diverted from its course, or causing splits, particularly on curves. The carver will find that by turning the work to favour the knife he can cut with confidence and avoid these problems.

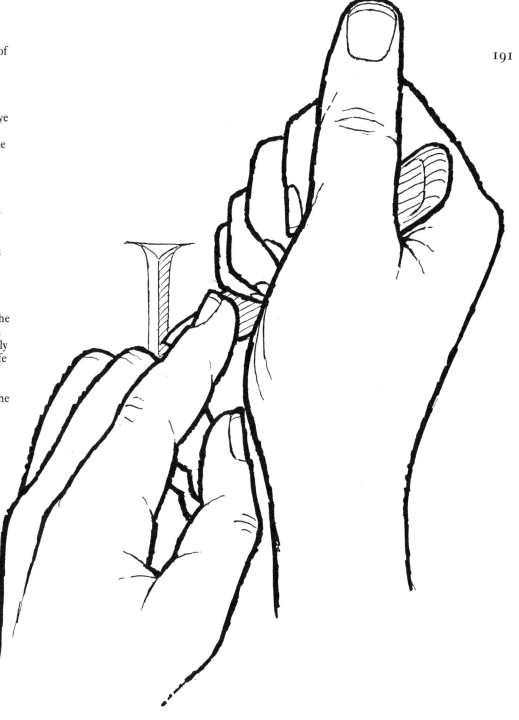

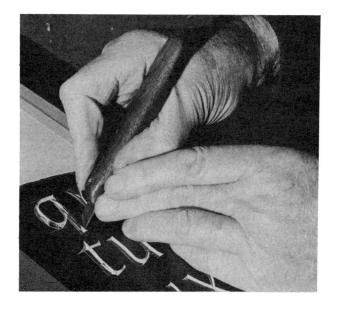

Relief carving

Letters to be carved in relief should first be outlined with a narrow gouge as shown here, keeping a little outside the drawn letter to allow for the later final shaping. The channel thus cut will isolate the letter from the background which can be carved back to the desired depth using suitable gouges. A hand-held power router is a useful tool for quickly lowering backgrounds to a constant depth. The final shaping of the letters is done with chisels and gouges, carving inside shapes first and leaving stroke ends to last so that any accidental damage may be cut back. A narrow gouge may be used to soften the angle where the letter meets the background, removing the myriad cuts left by the chisel. It is impossible to obtain a perfectly flat and smooth background so work this with a flattish gouge to give a slightly uneven surface. A gouge with a bent shaft will be helpful here. The sectional drawings below show these stages clearly.

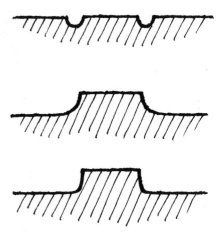

Finishes

The usual finishes for protecting wood are polyurethane varnish, wax polish and linseed oil, and stains may be used to darken or colour before the finish is applied. For outside use varnish is best, although oil may be used on teak too. Varnish is available in gloss, semi-gloss and matt. The light sheen of matt varnish is very attractive. Gloss is best reserved for outside work. Use a good brush and avoid dust.

Remember that the first application of varnish will raise the grain of wood, which will have to be rubbed down before the next coat is applied. For this reason it is best not to varnish relief carvings, unless they are to go outside, because it is difficult to rub down the carved surfaces without impairing their

quality. If this is necessary use a fine grade wire wool. Waxing, which does not affect the grain, should be done with a good beeswax furniture cream rubbed into the wood and polished off when dry.

Linseed oil will enrich hard woods such as oak and teak, giving the grain greater prominence. Brush well into the wood, or rub in with a cloth pad.

If the incised letters are to be painted apply a sealing coat first, then further coats of colour. Varnish can be applied as a final coat over the wood and the letters. The matt finish of Plaka paint, already recommended for use with stone, is equally suited to wood.

Three-dimensional letters

Free-standing letters in wood are an
obvious next stage and best done with
the aid of power tools such as routers
and bandsaws. The examples here
show several techniques and letter
styles. The monolithic E, carved from
a piece of end-grain elm, with its
scooped out face, deep recesses and
strong serifs is a development of the
nineteenth-century Egyptian letter.
Laminations and a stencil form
meant that R could be built up from
several layers cut from plywood with a
bandsaw. Each lamination was stained
in a different colour.

The name Pat, cut from a piece of
Parana pine with a bandsaw, shows the
importance of inner shapes in a design
of linked letters and the opening of 'a'
and P to allow access to the saw blade.
It is also clear that the design must be
bold enough to avoid splits along the
grain. The initial G, carved in pine and
gilded recalls the once common three-
dimensional wooden scripts seen on
nineteenth-century shopfronts. To
avoid splitting in letters of this kind it
is essential to seal the back of the wood
so that it is impervious to changes in
climatic conditions.

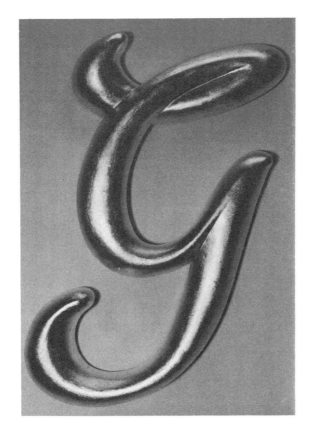

Slate is an attractive material for making paperweights and ideal for small lettering and the flourishes that can add an individual touch to a monogram, as in FG. It is fairly easy to shape, removing corners with a hacksaw to make an octagonal shape, MH, or with many more cuts and rubbing to make an oval, GK. These small pieces need clamping on a bench or may be temporarily glued to a piece of wood that can be attached to the easel or bench before carving can start. Darkening the slate by oiling will reduce the likelihood of disfiguring fingerprints.

Housenames may be of slate, stone or wood. When using lowercase letters position the name visually in the middle of the rectangle, allowing plenty of space beneath, even if, as in Strode Room, there are no descending strokes. The addition of a borderline will emphasise the shape of the nameplate, as in Annick Bank, which also uses a balancing swash on the B to complement the two ks on the right. The stone for 4 Valley Road combines a large figure and capitals on a curve in a strong, legible carving, painted to increase definition on a north-facing wall. Remember that housenames should be easy to read—the visitor searching for your house on a dark night will not appreciate illegible letters.

A brick-sized slate carrying a bold monogram, carved in a flat shallow section with light incised figures, provides a neat way of including the architect's initials and construction date in a building's fabric.

Strode Room

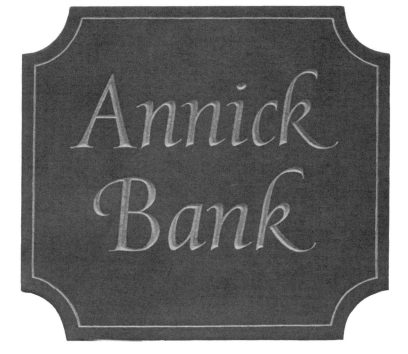

Annick Bank

4 VALLEY ROAD

1972

Public inscriptions, particularly memorials, are traditionally sober in design, should respect their environment and should not be an occasion for eccentricity in either letterform or layout. They are essentially records of persons or events and need only present the information clearly and elegantly, using good letterforms and suitable materials. The text, too, needs to be clear and concise and as free as possible from unnecessary detail and sentiment. In designing the gravestone described here, its site in a village churchyard, surrounded by eighteenth-century memorials, suggested a sympathetic centred arrangement of capitals and italic to provide clear articulation of a complex text. The first sketch, reproduced below, included the full

punctuation appropriate to continuous text but this is unnecessary in display lines where changes of letter style and line breaks make most commas and full stops redundant, so punctuation was minimised in the final design. A similar reduction in punctuation would have improved the memorial to Canon Clarke on page 199.

The long first line begins with a discreetly flourished capital that echoes the curve of the final f, while lower down a pause is made before the last two lines of italic and again before the final lines of italic capitals. Such pauses are helpful to the reader as well as being visually effective. Enough space is left below the inscription to allow for the grass that may grow high if the grave is not well kept, while a gently curved top and good margins set off

the lines of lettering. A design must meet the approval of the client and any authorities that may be concerned before work can proceed.

Full-size drawings made on strips of paper were pinned up to allow the design to be studied at actual size and any spacing problems resolved before transfer to the stone. Here the ninth line is too close in length to the line below and needs shortening very slightly.

The shaping of the three-inch-thick piece of Portland limestone was done by a skilled mason, allowing an extra twelve inches to go into the ground. Guidelines were drawn with a hard pencil and the lettering drawn directly onto the stone with a softer pencil using the previously drawn strip as a guide, making further improvements to

spacing while doing so. Alternatively the lettering could have been transferred with carbon paper. Cutting must begin at the bottom so that the pencil work is not erased, and because they must withstand the weather the letters need to be deeply and boldly cut. The deep shadows of these strong letters will also make them more legibile.

When the work was complete and the stone washed over to remove dust and any remaining pencil marks it was ready to be erected. The size and weight of a large gravestone means that this is a job for an expert, preferably a local mason who knows the particular churchyard. In the case of plaques that need to be fixed to walls the carver may wish to do this work himself, fixing non-ferrous metal dowels in holes in the back of the plaque with an epoxy resin adhesive and similarly securing the dowels in holes in the wall. If in any doubt about fixing heavy plaques always employ a skilled mason.

of your charity
Pray for
Nicholas Charles
Nicole
2 LT. 4/7 D.G.
of Slape Manor,
killed by an avalanche
27 March 1978
aged 20 years

In this gravestone
a deep moulding provides a strong setting
for elegant italic and roman letters which include
restrained flourishes.

Remember with gratitude and love
Basil Fulford Lowther Clarke, M.A.,
Hon. Canon of Christ Church, Oxford,
and for 30 years Vicar of Knowl Hill.
Born 6 March 1908, died 27 January 1978.

Capital letters are often specified for memorial tablets, but this legible slate inscription
of mainly lowercase letters shows another approach.

BENJAMIN BRITTEN 1913-1976

Condensed letters allow tall characters in the restricted space
of this inscription under a memorial window.

GOLDEN CAP
Given by members of The National Trust
and friends in memory of
THE EARL OF ANTRIM K.B.E.
Chairman of The National Trust
from 1966 until his death in 1977

Tough Cumbrian slate was used
in this plaque on an exposed coastal site in Dorset.
Such inscriptions must withstand both
the weather and the vandal.

THIS
MAZE WAS
DEDICATED BY
ROBERT RUNCIE
ARCHBISHOP OF
CANTERBURY
24 OCTOBER
1981

The words naturally
fit this diamond-shaped piece of Welsh slate
without breaks or hyphenation —
a happy circumstance.

ANNO·MILLESIMO·NON
GENTESIMO·SEXAGESIMO
SEPTIMO·DIE·SEXTO·MENSIS
NOVEMBRIS·QVI·DIES·NATALIS
EST·VNIVERSITATIS·LEODIENSIS
CENTVM·QVINQVAGINTA
ABHINC·ANNOS·CONDITAE
AEDIFICIA·QVAE·PRIMA·IN
PRAEDIO·EXSTRVCTA·SVNT
QVOD·SART·TILMAN·VOCATVR
INAVGVRATA·SVNT·A·BALDVINO
BELGARVM·REGE·MARCELLO
DVBVISSON·RECTORE

A latin inscription
marking the opening of the new university buildings at Liège
in Belgium uses capital letters en masse
in the classical roman manner, the lines arranged informally.
Carved in a very hard chunk of undressed stone
these letters lack the polish and elegant serifs of those
in the inscription shown opposite.

Sundial designs

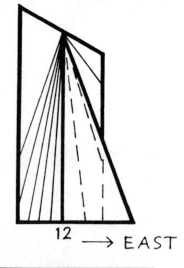

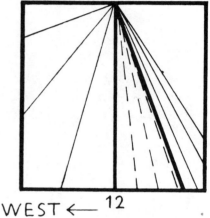

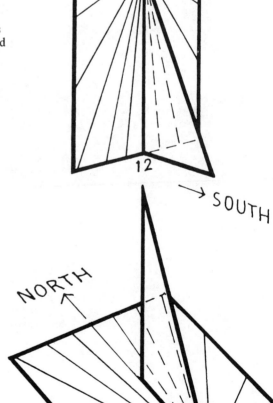

Inscriptions and sundials have a long association which continues today, even though sundials only agree exactly with the clock four times a year – 21 March, 21 June, 23 September and 21 December. During Summer Time the sundial will be approximately one hour slow. It has to be remembered that clock time is a convention whereby we agree that across a certain zone many miles wide it will be 12 noon, say, at the same moment, whereas true noon as shown by the sun is moving across the zone from east to west and is recorded at different moments on sundials as the sun passes.

A sundial may take many forms but here only simple horizontal and vertical designs are described. The essential parts of a sundial are the dial which is marked with hour-lines and the gnomon which throws the shadow on to the dial. Before any sundial can be designed it is essential to know the latitude of its position, and if it is a vertical dial its southerly orientation. Horizontal dials must be level and the 12 noon line carefully orientated to true north. A magnetic compasss gives only an approximate reading.

The basic facts governing sundial design are shown in the diagrams below. A line projected through the earth's surface marks the latitude (here 56 degrees for southern Scotland), the sun's rays come from the right, the horizontal dial is at right angles to the projected line, i.e. level with the earth's surface at that point and the right-

angled triangle of the gnomon is set on the dial at 56 degrees, the angle of latitude, its hypotenuse facing the sun (1). A vertical dial facing due south will be in line with the projected line, i.e. at a right-angle with the earth's surface, and the angle between its face and the gnomon's hypotenuse will be the angle of co-latitude, here 34 degrees (2). Vertical dials that do not face due south are said to be declining. A west-declining dial is shown (3) and east-declining (4). In all cases the gnomon's position is unchanged.

The plotting of hour-lines is described on the opposite page but this group of illustrations shows their disposition on the dials already described. Starting at the bottom the horizontal dial's gnomon is set on the noon-line which is orientated to the north, while the other hour-lines spread equally either side. Above this is the vertical dial facing due south, hour-lines equally disposed either side of the gnomon as on the horizontal dial, although at different angles. Next the west-declining dial, its face turned towards the reader, shows the morning hour-lines to the left of the gnomon widely spread and the afternoon hour-lines becoming tightly packed while this situation is reversed in the east-declining dial shown at the top. In each instance the gnomon remains orientated on the north-south axis and its angle, determined by the angle of latitude, remains the same.

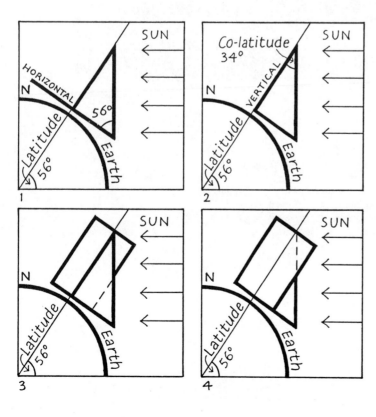

The methods for plotting hour-lines for horizontal, vertical and declining sundials described here have been adapted from *Practical Directions for the Construction and Fixing of Sundials (1889)* and if followed carefully will produce accurate results.

Horizontal

Draw triangle ABC, AB vertical, angle ABC same as latitude, angle BCA = 90°. Draw line AD same length as AC and line AE horizontally from A. From D draw radiating lines at 15° intervals to meet line AE. Lines drawn from B to meet these points are the hour-lines 1–5 pm. 12 noon is A and 6 is horizontal from B. Repeat on left for hour-lines 6–11 am. Hour-lines before 6 am and after 6 pm may be projected from the lines already drawn, 7 am to 7 pm instance. Continue BC to meet line AE at F. AF is the height of the gnomon that is required to plot the hour-lines on a vertical dial as described below.

Vertical

To find the hour-lines for a vertical dial facing due south first draw the diagram for a horizontal dial as described above, with AE extended left and marked with hour positions from 7 am to 5 pm. From A draw the vertical line AG to give the height of the gnomon (this line's length is the same as AF in the diagram for a horizontal dial). From G draw downwards radiating lines to meet the hour positions on line AE. The horizontal running through G provides the 6 am, 6 pm line, while lines for hours before and after these times may be projected from the existing hour-lines, as already described for horizontal dials.

Declining

If the wall to which the sundial is to be fixed does not face due south measure with a compass and protractor the degree to which it declines east or west. The illustration shows a west-declining dial of 30°. Draw the diagram for a horizontal dial showing hour-lines from 6 am to 6 pm, then draw line HK through A (the 12 noon point) at 30° to the extended line AE. Extend the hour-lines on the left and mark the meeting points on line HK, both left and right. A similar method will be necessary for an east-declining dial, with the hour-lines on the right extended to meet line HK. Now proceed as already described for a vertical dial, substituting line HK horizontally for AE. If the degree of declination is great some of these hour-lines may not appear on the dial face.

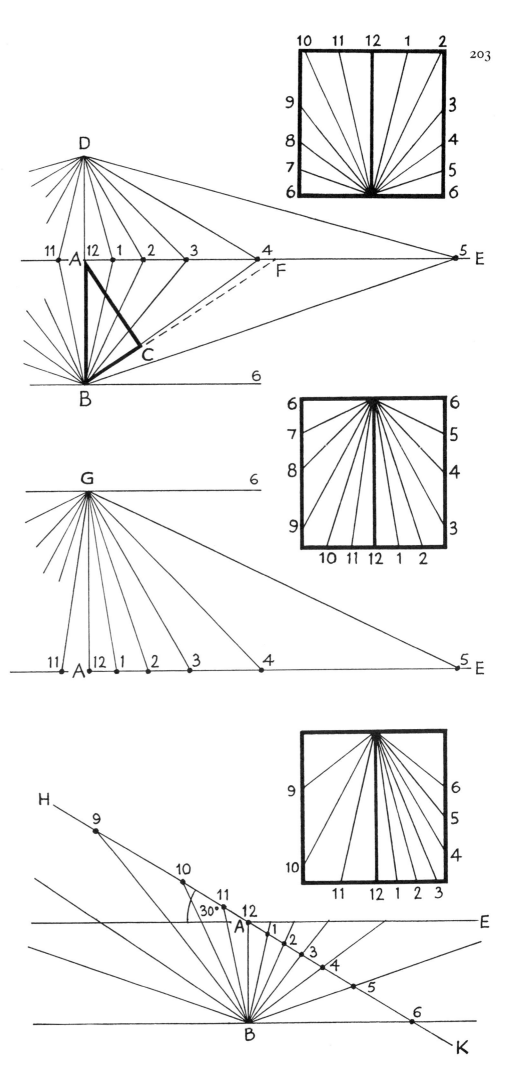

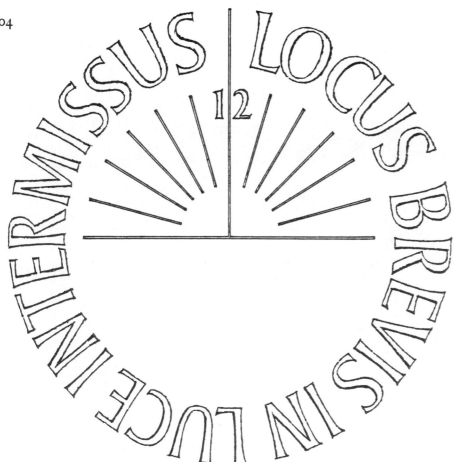

Slate sundial

Conceived by Ian Hamilton Finlay this large sundial was made in collaboration with him for the University of Liège in Belgium. The four-foot diameter riven slate mounted on a cast concrete base and surrounded by a circle of paving is sited on a university campus that is famed for its modern buildings and natural landscaping. Large, strong letters were necessary on the uneven surface of the slate, and the slightly condensed capitals form a well integrated circle. The latin text translates as *A small interruption in the light*.

The actual sundial is treated very simply with only 12 noon being indicated, while the gnomon is a plain bronze triangle.

Garden sundial

This sundial designed for the wall of a
house with a southerly aspect declines
10° to the west. It is made of Welsh
slate, and the gnomon is shaped from
stainless steel.

The text, a child's imaginative
reaction to a cloud-filled sky, reminds
the frustrated time-seeker that clouds
have a positive attribute. Rounded italic
letters provide a decorative and
expressive word pattern that floats
above the simple sundial. Being made
in two pieces this sundial could be
moved to another site, and the lower
piece remade to suit the new location.

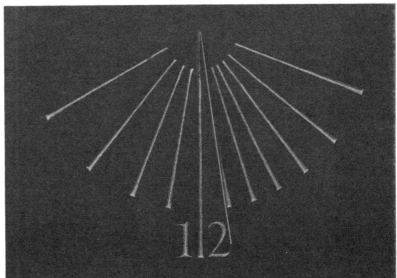

Relief carving in oak

An exhibition piece gives the designer unusual freedom in the choice of words, material and format. This wood carving was shown at the exhibition held at the University of Texas at Austin to celebrate the 150th anniversary of William Morris's birth.

The quotation from Morris has long delighted the author and the design was conceived as an obviously contemporary piece—the lettering ranged left—and Morris's enthusiasm for the Middle Ages is reflected in the condensed forms reminiscent of blackletter. English oak provided an apt material and the tall, narrow shape, perhaps suggesting a totem pole, reinforces the stern commanding tone of Morris's admonition.

Most of the waste material was removed with a router, the letters carved as illustrated on the opposite page and the background worked over with a flattish gouge to give a contrast with the finely sanded surface of the letters. Wax polish added the finishing touch to this homage to a great thinker and craftsman.

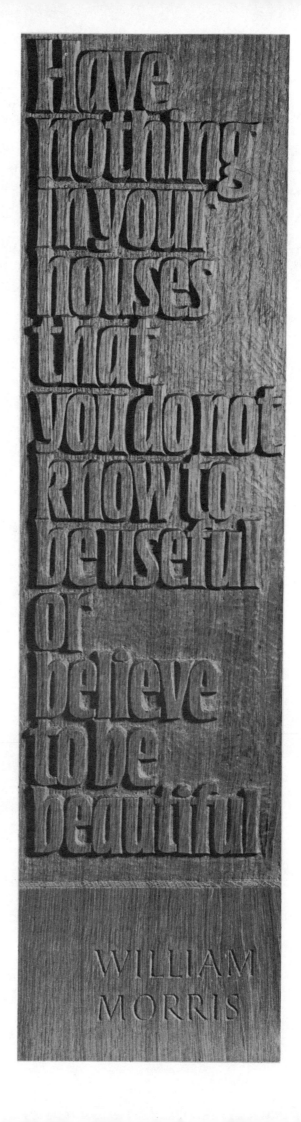

Carved and painted alphabet in pine

Power tools enable a designer to attempt carvings that would otherwise be extremely tedious. The bold, informal letters (shown full size below) in this experimental piece were carved in a rough-surfaced length of Parana pine with the help of a hand-held power router, following the sequence illustrated opposite.

The design was drawn onto the masking tape used to protect the surface, then each letter was cut out with a craft knife and peeled off. Routing was done using an $\frac{1}{8}$ inch cutter keeping just inside the letter and

a $\frac{1}{4}$ inch cutter to remove the remaining material. The depth was set at $\frac{1}{8}$ inch for the first routing operation, then lowered to $\frac{1}{4}$ inch to reach the final depth; see sectional drawings below.

Finished carving of the letters with hand tools removed the rough edges left by the router, and the corners where the letters' sides meet the bottom were rounded off with a narrow U-shaped gouge. After painting with yellow Plaka the tape was peeled off, revealing strong, smooth, deeply shadowed letters contrasting with the rough sawn texture of the wood.

Two alphabets incised in slate

Collectors of fine lettering sometimes commission alphabets from letter carvers, providing them with a greater challenge than is usually offered by clients. The carver feels that each letter is a definitive statement, his last word on that form, that every serif must be of breath-taking finesse and the possibility of perfection is within his grasp. In short, his skill and artistry are on trial. For this reason it takes considerably longer to carve an alphabet than it does to carve twenty-six similar letterforms in a more routine job, in a gravestone for instance. Perversely enough the best letters are often carved quickly, when the experienced carver is working to a deadline, free from anxiety about his performance.

These two alphabets, designed to be seen together, show the kind of italic and roman letters that the author has been carving and drawing for many years. His early devotion to the work of Eric Gill and long association with Reynolds Stone is evident in these letters, although they are not copies of any master's work. Rather they are to be seen as a personal affirmation and continuation of the tradition of letters that goes back to the Renaissance and the Roman period, flourishing still in the hands of such contemporary masters as Hermann Zapf and John Benson.

ABC
DEFGHIJ
KLMN
OPQRST
UVWX
Y&Z

A child's alphabet incised in pine

The letterforms in this alphabet for a young child are less austere than the classical roman capitals on the preceding page. They are strongly carved, with the child's initials in a larger size, and painted in red and orange. Designed to be handled, the block of Parana pine is rounded off on all edges and corners to eliminate splinters, and finished with glossy polyurethane varnish to ensure maximum protection in the hurly-burly of the toy cupboard.

Relief carving in Purbeck stone

Rowena Cade's open air theatre among the cliffs at Minack in Cornwall was largely built by her own hands over a period of many years, so the stone set into the rocks to record this fact uses rugged letters that reflect the character of the place. The bold relief capitals are closely grouped to achieve maximum impact in this wild setting. The background roughened with a point tool creates a strong contrast and improves legibility, which might otherwise be impaired by the closely grouped letters.

The laborious task of lowering the background in this block of Purbeck stone was done by a trade mason using a pneumatically powered chisel to follow a carefully drawn outline of the letters, an example of sensible collaboration between designer and skilled workman.

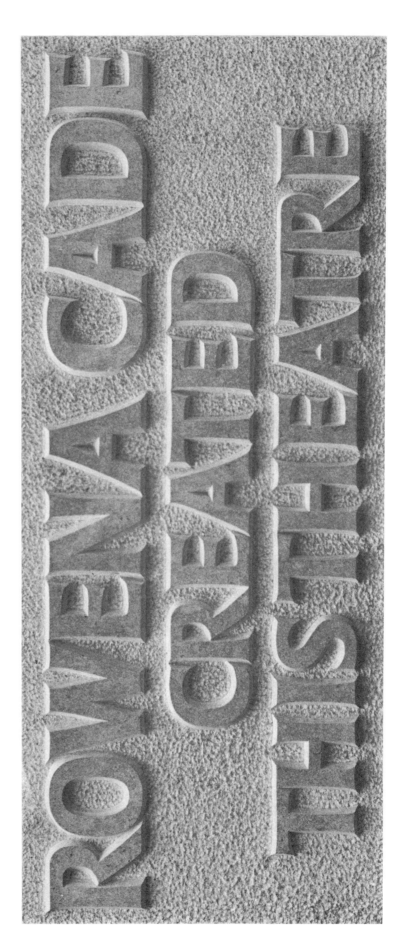

Wood pattern for bronze casting

Three bronze figures by Elisabeth Frink commemorate Catholic martyrs persecuted under Elizabeth I at Dorchester, Dorset where this public memorial is placed. The ancient technique of casting in a sand mould was used to produce the bronze plaque set in the paving between these figures. Arranging the short text within a circle required flexible letterforms in varying heights that would complement the Frink figures and stand up to the wear and tear of the elements and pedestrian traffic.

Each letter was drawn on paper in outline and fixed to ¼ inch plywood with spray adhesive, then cut out on a power bandsaw to make a pattern for the sand mould, the saw set to provide a 5-degree slope or draft on the edge to facilitate removal from the mould. Each letter was hand-finished with rasps, files and fine sandpaper before being glued and pinned into place on the 24-inch diameter base. Protective coats of varnish were applied before the pattern was sent to the foundry.

The finished casting's highly polished letters (shown full-sized, right) read well against the darkened background.

Large-scale letters in stone

Several large inscriptions in the Sains-bury Wing, Robert Venturi's extension to London's National Gallery, required very careful planning and a different approach to the design and carving process: letters above a certain size have to be treated as sculpture. The largest inscription, a line of artists' names – DUCCIO·MASACCIO·VAN EYCK·PIERO· MANTEGNA·BELLINI·LEONARDO·RAPHAEL – used capital letters half a metre high, while in others sizes ranged from 185 to 325 millimetres. Letterforms, far from the style of the classical Roman capitals on page 10, were developed from typo-graphic letters contemporary with the 1830 original building, having strong serifs, a marked contrast in stroke weight and slightly condensed proportions.

Drawings of each letter were enlarged to full-size then transferred to card to make templates, below, and a scale lay-out drawing established letter and word spacing.

On site, accurate guide lines were drawn on the surface of the limestone blocks, the position of each letter deter-mined from the scaled-up layout, before they were outlined in crayon using the templates as a guide. On stone, crayon rubs off less easily than pencil. Scale drawings are not infallible, and some adjustments were required on the full-size layout before carving could begin.

Each letter was outlined with a vee-cut; then, where joints ran through the letter, a chisel was used to cut down into the stone, removing material that could easily break away later (see illustration opposite, top left). The bulk of the stone was removed with a claw tool, driven by a mallet, as shown opposite, top right.

A protective mask is essential during these dusty operations. Carving with a chisel completed each letter.

In the photograph opposite, letters on the front of the building are shown partly finished, while the lower photo-graph shows most of this inscription. Notice the placing of the lines towards the top of the blocks, to be visually less confined by the grid, and the care taken to minimise interference by vertical joints.

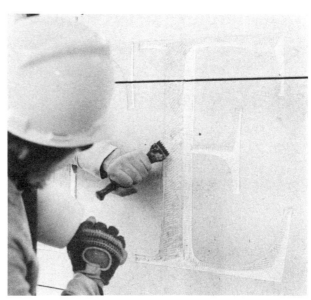

Sculptured alphabet in pine

The alphabet as an art object is a fairly recent idea, a development perhaps of writing masters' and type manu-facturers' specimen books which presented alphabets as models for writing or as desirable additions to a printer's range of styles. The designer working closely with letters is always aware of their abstract beauty and sometimes moved to express this in the pure, wordless form of an alphabet.

This example, made from Parana pine with the help of a bandsaw and router, exploits the outline of free-standing form and the shadows of deeply recessed spaces between and inside closely packed letters. The original design did not include the ampersand; it was added to provide a contrasting element among the diagonals of the bottom line.

Beeswax gives a lustre to the carved wood and darkens the base of Welsh slate. Good lighting is the final requirement if this sculpture is to be seen at its best.

ABCabc
DEFdef
GHIghi
JKLjkl
MN mn
OPQopq
RSTrst
UVWuvw
XYZxyz

Postscript and bibliography

Calligraphy is a frequent touchstone throughout this book, and rightly so, since whether drawn, carved or digitized letters, their forms can be traced back to writing. Therefore some practical experience with the pen is recommended, and those wanting to take their studies further should turn to some of the books in the bibliography that follows.

To describe a skill in words and pictures is very difficult. It is easier to learn by practice than by reading. Remember that skill is at the service of form, that the skill shown by, say, a master carving letters in stone is similar to that of a high-wire artist who crosses a chasm without faltering, producing gasps of amazement in the onlooker. The sight of the carver's chisel cutting a line without wobbling may also cause amazement, but it should be remembered that this skill is only a means to an end, the carving of beautiful letters.

The difference between the novice and the master, whether carving, writing, drawing or digitizing, is this: the novice concentrates on the process while the master concentrates on the letter. Skills are slowly acquired together with the confidence to forget the tool and consider only the letter's shape.

The design of lettering involves many factors apart from letterforms. Working to commission means an acceptance of limitations, which should only be a spur to creativity. The words can rarely be changed, the format may be fixed, but the designer seeks the most effective arrangement of letters to arrive at what should appear to be the only possible solution to each problem, a challenge to his skill, knowledge and imagination.

All the lettering in this book came from the author's hand, and reflects to some degree his personality. Those who attempt a similar commitment to the making of letters may find, with time, their own style and voice.

Bibliography

Hermann Zapf: *Creative Calligraphy*, Hamburg 1985

Published by the Rotring company in Germany in conjunction with their Artpen range of pens. Zapf's text and examples are all that one would expect from this master of twentieth-century calligraphy. Available from Artpen suppliers or John Neal, Bookseller, 1833 Spring Garden Street, Greensboro, NC 27403, USA.

Karlgeorg Hoefer: *Kalligraphie*, Düsseldorf 1986

A useful and compact introduction to pen and brush writing by a master practitioner. An English translation is included. Available from John Neal (see above).

Susanne Haines: *The Calligrapher's Project Book*, London 1987

Mainly for calligraphers, this book presents in more detail some of the techniques described in the present volume. Explores graphic uses of calligraphy.

Albert Kapr: *The Art of Lettering*, Munich, New York, London, Paris 1983

A scholarly text in English and several full-colour illustrations, tracing the history of lettering and type.

Edward M. Catich: *The Origin of the Serif*, Davenport 1968

Far more than the serif is discussed in this substantial volume. No other work so expertly and clearly demonstrates the role of brush writing in the construction of Roman capital letters.

Nicolete Gray: *Lettering as Drawing*, Oxford 1971

In this wide-ranging book Mrs Gray covers *art nouveau* as well as other less appreciated periods of creative lettering. Essential reading for all interested in calligraphy and lettering in their widest applications.

Ben Shahn: *Love and Joy About Letters*, London 1964

The autobiographical text describes Shahn's early training in drawing roman letters, 'I suppose that I spent months just on A alone'. He tells of his later discovery of American amateur hand-lettered signs. An inspirational collection of Shahn's very idiosyncratic lettering.

Michael Harvey: *Lettering Design* London and New York 1975

Covering many aspects of the design and use of letters, providing a useful introduction to contemporary lettering practice.

Erik Lindegren: *ABC of Lettering and Printing Types*, Sweden 1969

This book has many of its illustrations by twentieth-century designers, such as Hermann Zapf, Chris Brand and Adrian Frutiger, giving the historical forms a fresh interpretation.

Peter Karow: *Digital Formats for Typefaces*, Hamburg 1987

This book by the inventor of the IKARUS system of digital type generation is, as Hermann Zapf writes in his preface, aimed at both technicians in electronics and users of typefaces in many and varied applications.

Rosemary Sassoon: *Computers and Typography*, Oxford 1993

Essays ranging from the discussion of spacing and layout, education, and technical aspects of type design, showing that what has been learned in the past five centuries of traditional typography is still relevant in this computer era when, as Dr Sassoon says, letters of all kinds appear at the touch of a button.

Sepp Jakob and P. Donatus M. Leicher: *Schrift und Symbol*, München 1977

A German text, but the illustrations speak directly. This rich range of contemporary stone-carved lettering is much admired by English carvers trying to shake off their narrow traditions.

Alan Bartram: *Tombstone Lettering in the British Isles*, London 1978

This author's writings on lettering are always stimulating, particularly so in this book with its wealth of examples of 18th- and 19th-century gravestones.

John Howard Benson and Graham Carey: *Elements of Lettering*, Newport 1940

A sound and well illustrated book on the principles of lettering, unique among lettering books in providing instruction in wood-carving technique. Benson's son John is the finest inscription carver working in America today.

David Kindersley and Lida Lopes Cardozo: *Letters Slate Cut*, London 1981

Kindersley, once apprenticed to Eric Gill, was the best known English letter carver. This instructional book shows many examples of his work and is illustrated with Lida Lopes Cardozo's attractive drawings.

Edward Johnston: *Writing & Illuminating & Lettering*, London 1906

The Appendix by Eric Gill remains the clearest, concise description of the technique of carving letters in stone.

Richard Grasby: *Lettercutting in Stone*, Oswestry 1989

An exemplary presentation of carving methods, very well illustrated with the author's excellent drawings and photographs.

Rene R. J. Rhohr: *Sundials*, Toronto 1970

An elegant guide to the cosmography and mathematics of sundials.

Letter Arts Review

This quarterly publication covers all aspects of lettering, historical and contemporary, and reviews of books and exhibitions. Excellent illustrations abound in this quality journal, which is available by subscription from:
Letter Arts Review, 1624 24th Avenue SW, Norman, OK 73072, USA.

Index